AI4 Entrepreneurs

Revolutionize Your Business and Conquer Your Industry with AI

Jamie Culican

Melle Melkumian

Published by Dragon Realm Press

Cape May Court House, New Jersey, USA

www.dragonrealmpress.com

AI-Enabled Technology was utilized in collaboration when creating this series.

Printed in the USA

First Edition: May 23, 2023

Contents

INTRODUCTION

WELCOME TO THE ERA OF AI-DRIVEN ENTREPRENEURSHIP, where artificial intelligence is rapidly becoming the new frontier for innovation and growth in the world of small businesses. This book, "The AI-Powered Small Business: Harnessing Artificial Intelligence for Growth and Success," is designed to serve as a comprehensive guide for entrepreneurs who wish to explore the incredible potential of AI to transform their ventures and create a competitive edge in today's fast-paced business landscape.

In the past few years, AI has emerged as a powerful force in various industries, from healthcare to finance and logistics, making it more accessible and valuable to entrepreneurs than ever before. The ability of AI to automate tasks, optimize processes, and generate actionable insights makes it a game-changer for startups and small businesses. As an entrepreneur, harnessing AI's potential can help you save time, resources, and propel your business towards success.

Throughout this book, you will be introduced to the fundamentals of AI and its impact on modern businesses, focusing on the specific needs and challenges faced by entrepreneurs. You will learn about the many ways AI can enhance various aspects of your business operations, from marketing and sales to customer service and financial management. Additionally, we will delve into the risks and challenges associated with implementing AI, addressing concerns about privacy, security, and the ethical use of this powerful technology.

To help you make the most of AI for your business, this book provides practical advice on building an AI-driven business model, identifying the right tools and applications, and fostering a data-driven culture. We will also explore the legal and regulatory challenges of AI, hiring and training for AI-focused roles, and provide insights from successful AI-driven businesses that have navigated these challenges and reaped the rewards.

Finally, we will take a glimpse into the future of AI and entrepreneurship, examining emerging trends and developments that will continue to shape the business world in the years to come. Our goal is to equip you with the knowledge and confidence to embrace the potential of AI for your business, ensuring that you stay ahead of the curve and thrive in this exciting new era of entrepreneurship.

So, join us on this journey towards AI-powered growth

and success, and discover how you can leverage artificial intelligence to revolutionize your small business and create a lasting impact in your industry. Let's embark on this incredible adventure together and unleash the true potential of your entrepreneurial vision.

INTRODUCTION TO THE AI-POWERED SMALL BUSINESS: THE ENTREPRENEURIAL PERSPECTIVE ON AI

As an entrepreneur, you are constantly on the lookout for new and innovative ways to improve your business, gain a competitive advantage, and drive growth. In this rapidly evolving digital era, artificial intelligence (AI) has emerged as a powerful tool that has the potential to revolutionize the way businesses operate, making them more efficient, responsive, and agile. This section of the book, "The AI-Powered Small Business: The Entrepreneurial Perspective on AI," aims to provide you with a solid understanding of AI from an entrepreneurial standpoint and explore the immense possibilities that it holds for your venture.

AI is no longer confined to the realm of large corporations or cutting-edge research labs. Advances in technology and the democratization of AI tools have made it more accessible and affordable for small businesses and startups, empowering entrepreneurs like you to harness its transformative power. From automating mundane tasks and streamlining operations to predicting market trends and personalizing customer experiences, AI offers a myriad of opportunities to enhance the way you run your business and, ultimately, achieve your entrepreneurial goals.

In this section, we will delve into the core concepts and principles of AI, demystifying the jargon and unraveling the hype that surrounds this technology. You will learn about the various types of AI, such as machine learning, natural language processing, and computer vision, as well as the real-world applications that can benefit your business in a multitude of ways. We will also explore the unique challenges and opportunities that AI presents from an entrepreneurial perspective, including ethical considerations, data management, and the implications of AI on the future of work.

As an entrepreneur, your ability to adapt and embrace new technologies can determine the success or failure of your venture. This section will provide you with practical guidance on how to identify AI-powered solutions that align with your business goals, create a roadmap for AI implementation, and foster a culture of innovation and continuous learning within your organization. We will also discuss the importance of developing a data-driven mindset and the skills required to navigate the complex world of AI.

In essence, this section is designed to empower you with the knowledge and insights necessary to make informed decisions about AI adoption, and to help you leverage this game-changing technology to drive growth, increase efficiency, and achieve long-lasting success for your small business. Let's embark on this exciting journey together and discover how the entrepreneurial perspective on AI can shape the future of your venture and redefine the way you approach business.

EMPHASIZING THE POTENTIAL OF AI FOR STARTUPS AND SMALL BUSINESSES

In today's fast-paced and competitive business landscape, startups and small businesses must continually adapt and innovate to stay ahead. One of the most promising and transformative technologies at their disposal is artificial intelligence (AI). This section, "Emphasizing the Potential of AI for Startups and Small Businesses," highlights the immense opportunities that AI offers to entrepreneurs, demonstrating how it can serve as a catalyst for growth, efficiency, and innovation.

First and foremost, AI can help startups and small businesses level the playing field against larger competitors by enabling them to automate processes, optimize resources, and make more informed decisions. For instance, AI-powered tools can automate time-consuming tasks such as data entry, customer service, and inventory management, allowing small businesses to focus on their core competencies and allocate their resources more effectively. By reducing the burden of manual labor and increasing operational efficiency, AI empowers small businesses to scale rapidly and compete with more established players in their respective markets.

Another significant advantage of AI for startups and small businesses is its ability to generate actionable insights from vast amounts of data. By leveraging machine learning algorithms and advanced analytics, AI can help entrepreneurs identify trends, patterns, and opportunities that may otherwise go unnoticed. These insights can inform various aspects of a business, from product development and marketing strategies to pricing and inventory management. By harnessing the power of data-driven decision-making, small businesses can become more agile and responsive to market changes, allowing them to stay ahead of the competition.

AI can also play a crucial role in enhancing customer experiences, which is essential for building brand loyalty and driving growth. Personalized marketing campaigns, intelligent chatbots, and AI-driven product recommendations are just a few examples of how AI can help small businesses engage and retain customers more effectively. By leveraging AI to create personalized and seamless interactions, startups and small businesses can foster deeper connections with their customers, resulting in increased satisfaction, loyalty, and ultimately, revenue.

Furthermore, AI can contribute to the financial management aspect of small businesses by providing tools for cash flow forecasting, expense tracking, and fraud detection. By automating financial tasks and providing real-time insights,

AI enables entrepreneurs to make more informed financial decisions, ensuring the long-term sustainability and success of their ventures.

The potential of AI for startups and small businesses is immense, offering a wide array of opportunities to drive growth, efficiency, and innovation. As an entrepreneur, embracing AI and its transformative capabilities can help you gain a competitive edge, adapt to the ever-changing business landscape, and ultimately, achieve your entrepreneurial dreams. By emphasizing the potential of AI for your business, you are taking a crucial step towards securing a successful and prosperous future in the world of entrepreneurship.

THE IMPORTANCE OF EARLY AI ADOPTION FOR ENTREPRENEURS

As the world embraces the digital revolution, artificial intelligence (AI) has emerged as a groundbreaking technology that is transforming industries across the globe. For entrepreneurs, staying ahead of the curve and capitalizing on emerging trends is crucial for success. This section, titled "The Importance of Early AI Adoption for Entrepreneurs," highlights the benefits of adopting AI early on and explains why entrepreneurs should seize the opportunity to integrate AI into their businesses now, rather than later.

By embracing AI early on, entrepreneurs can gain a competitive advantage and establish themselves as pioneers

in their respective industries. AI can help businesses optimize operations, streamline processes, and enhance
customer experiences, leading to increased efficiency,
productivity, and profitability. Early AI adopters can set
themselves apart from their competitors and demonstrate
their commitment to innovation, attracting customers and
investors alike.

Another reason for early AI adoption is the potential for
rapid scaling. AI-powered tools and applications can help
automate various aspects of a business, allowing entrepreneurs to scale up their operations quickly and efficiently. By
integrating AI into their business models, entrepreneurs can
focus on growth and expansion, while AI takes care of the
mundane and repetitive tasks that would otherwise consume
valuable time and resources.

Early AI adoption also enables entrepreneurs to develop
a data-driven mindset and culture within their organizations. As AI relies on large amounts of data to function
effectively, businesses must prioritize data collection,
management, and analysis. By embracing AI from the
outset, entrepreneurs can instill a data-centric approach
throughout their organizations, leading to better decision-
making and a more resilient business model.

Furthermore, integrating AI early on can help entrepreneurs mitigate risks and identify potential challenges before
they become major roadblocks. AI can provide valuable
insights into market trends, customer preferences, and operational inefficiencies, allowing entrepreneurs to address

potential issues proactively. By incorporating AI into their risk management strategies, entrepreneurs can make more informed decisions and navigate the complex business landscape with confidence.

Finally, early AI adoption can help entrepreneurs build and retain a talented workforce. As AI continues to gain prominence, businesses that embrace AI are more likely to attract top talent who are interested in working with cutting-edge technologies. Additionally, by automating repetitive tasks, entrepreneurs can empower their employees to focus on more creative and strategic endeavors, resulting in increased job satisfaction and a more engaged workforce.

The importance of early AI adoption for entrepreneurs cannot be overstated. By embracing AI now, entrepreneurs can position themselves as industry leaders, streamline operations, scale rapidly, develop a data-driven culture, mitigate risks, and attract top talent. By seizing the opportunity to harness the transformative power of AI, entrepreneurs can set the stage for long-term success and solidify their place in the ever-evolving world of business.

BOOK SETUP AND EXPECTATIONS: YOUR GUIDE TO AI-POWERED ENTREPRENEURSHIP

As we embark on this journey through the world of artificial intelligence (AI) and its impact on entrepreneurship, it is important to establish the book's setup and the expectations you, as a reader, can have as you delve deeper into the content. This section, titled "Book Setup and Expectations: Your Guide to AI-Powered Entrepreneurship," aims to provide an overview of the structure and content of the book, while setting the stage for a comprehensive understanding of AI's potential for startups and small businesses.

The book is organized into several key sections, each designed to build upon the previous one, providing a well-rounded and progressive exploration of AI in the context of entrepreneurship. We begin by introducing the fundamentals of AI, including its history, key concepts, and technologies. This foundational knowledge will set the stage for the rest of the book, ensuring that you have a solid understanding of AI and its underlying principles.

Following the introduction, we delve into the benefits and challenges of integrating AI into your business. This section will provide a balanced perspective on the potential advantages of AI, as well as the risks and ethical considerations involved in its implementation. You will gain insights into how AI can improve efficiency, productivity, and customer experiences, while also addressing concerns related to data privacy, security, and the displacement of human labor.

Next, we explore practical applications of AI across various aspects of business operations, such as marketing, sales, customer service, product development, and financial management. Each chapter focuses on a specific area of business, discussing relevant AI-powered tools and strategies that can help entrepreneurs streamline processes and drive growth. Real-world examples and case studies will be provided throughout the book, illustrating how other businesses have successfully leveraged AI to achieve their objectives.

As we progress through the book, we also tackle the legal and regulatory challenges associated with AI, as well as strategies for hiring and training an AI-ready workforce. These sections will help entrepreneurs navigate the complexities of AI implementation while ensuring compliance with applicable laws and fostering a culture of innovation within their organizations.

Finally, we conclude with an outlook on the future of AI in entrepreneurship, highlighting emerging trends, technologies, and opportunities for innovation. This forward-looking perspective will equip entrepreneurs with the knowledge and inspiration needed to adapt and thrive in the rapidly evolving world of AI.

Throughout the book, our goal is to provide you with a comprehensive, engaging, and informative guide to AI-powered entrepreneurship. By the end, you can expect to have a solid understanding of AI's potential for your business, along with actionable insights and strategies to help you harness this transformative technology and drive success in today's competitive landscape.

CHAPTER 1

ENTREPRENEURIAL MINDSET AND AI: EMBRACING INNOVATION FOR BUSINESS SUCCESS

As an entrepreneur, the ability to adapt and embrace change is essential for the growth and success of your business. In this section, titled "Entrepreneurial Mindset and AI: Embracing Innovation for Business Success," we explore the importance of cultivating an entrepreneurial mindset when approaching the adoption of artificial intelligence (AI) in your business.

The entrepreneurial mindset is characterized by qualities such as curiosity, resilience, adaptability, and a strong drive for innovation. These traits are particularly relevant when it comes to embracing AI, as this technology has the potential to reshape entire industries, redefine business models, and unlock new opportunities for growth. By approaching AI with an entrepreneurial mindset, you can better position your business to capitalize on these opportunities and stay ahead of the competition.

One key aspect of the entrepreneurial mindset is the willingness to experiment and learn from failures. AI is a rapidly evolving field, and its applications are still being explored and refined. As you begin to integrate AI into your business, it is crucial to maintain a spirit of experimentation, allowing yourself to test various AI-driven solutions and strategies, and learning from the results. This willingness to iterate and learn from failures can ultimately help you uncover the most effective ways to leverage AI for your business.

Another critical element of the entrepreneurial mindset is the ability to recognize and seize new opportunities. As AI continues to advance, it will inevitably give rise to new business models, markets, and customer needs. Entrepreneurs who can identify these opportunities early on and adapt their businesses accordingly will be best positioned for success in the AI-driven economy.

Lastly, embracing AI as an entrepreneur also involves fostering a culture of continuous learning and innovation within your organization. AI is a complex and rapidly evolving field, and staying informed about the latest developments is essential to making informed decisions about its integration into your business. Encouraging a culture of learning and curiosity among your employees will help ensure that your business remains agile and adaptable as AI continues to transform the business landscape.

Adopting an entrepreneurial mindset when approaching AI can significantly enhance your ability to harness its potential for your business. By fostering curiosity, adaptability, resilience, and a focus on innovation, you can better position your business to capitalize on the opportunities presented by AI, drive growth, and achieve lasting success in the AI-powered future.

Cultivating an Innovation-Focused Mindset: Unlocking the Potential of AI for Entrepreneurial Success

In the dynamic world of business, an innovation-focused mindset is a key determinant of success, especially when integrating emerging technologies like artificial intelligence (AI) into your business model. In this section, titled "Cultivating an Innovation-Focused Mindset: Unlocking the Potential of AI for Entrepreneurial Success," we explore the importance of nurturing a culture of innovation within your organization and how it can help you harness the full potential of AI for your business.

An innovation-focused mindset involves embracing change, encouraging creative thinking, and fostering an environment that supports continuous learning and improvement. By cultivating such a mindset within your organization, you can better adapt to the rapid advancements in AI technology and stay ahead of the curve in your industry.

Here are some key strategies for fostering an innovation-focused mindset in your business:

1. ENCOURAGE CURIOSITY AND CREATIVE THINKING: Create a culture where employees feel comfortable asking questions, challenging assumptions, and proposing novel ideas. Encourage cross-functional collaboration and provide opportunities for employees to learn about AI and other emerging technologies. This will help them develop a deeper understanding of the potential applications of AI within your business and inspire creative thinking around new ways to leverage AI for growth.

2. PROMOTE EXPERIMENTATION AND LEARNING FROM Failures: Encourage a culture of experimentation by providing the resources and support needed for employees to test and refine their AI-driven ideas. Recognize that failures are an essential part of the innovation process and create an environment where employees feel comfortable learning from their mistakes. This will help them to iterate quickly and ultimately develop more effective AI-driven solutions for your business.

3. INVEST IN CONTINUOUS LEARNING AND SKILL Development: As AI continues to evolve, staying informed

about the latest developments and trends is essential for success. Provide opportunities for your employees to participate in workshops, conferences, and online courses related to AI and other emerging technologies. Investing in the continuous learning and skill development of your workforce will help ensure that your organization remains agile and adaptable as the AI landscape evolves.

4. FOSTER COLLABORATION AND KNOWLEDGE SHARING: Encourage open communication and knowledge sharing within your organization. Create platforms and channels where employees can share their ideas, insights, and experiences related to AI and other innovative technologies. This will help to stimulate creative thinking, facilitate cross-functional collaboration, and create a more cohesive and informed team that can better leverage AI for business success.

5. RECOGNIZE AND REWARD INNOVATION: REINFORCE THE importance of innovation by recognizing and rewarding employees who contribute to the development and implementation of AI-driven solutions. This will help to motivate your workforce, foster a sense of ownership, and ensure that innovation remains a top priority within your organization.

. . .

CULTIVATING AN INNOVATION-FOCUSED MINDSET WITHIN your organization is crucial for unlocking the full potential of AI for your business. By embracing change, encouraging creative thinking, and fostering a culture of continuous learning and improvement, you can position your business to capitalize on the opportunities presented by AI and drive lasting success in the increasingly competitive business landscape.

EMBRACING TECHNOLOGY AS A CATALYST FOR GROWTH: HARNESSING AI AND DIGITAL INNOVATION FOR ENTREPRENEURIAL SUCCESS

In today's rapidly evolving business landscape, embracing technology is no longer an option, but a necessity for entrepreneurs who want to remain competitive and achieve sustainable growth. In this section, titled "Embracing Technology as a Catalyst for Growth: Harnessing AI and Digital Innovation for Entrepreneurial Success," we explore the importance of adopting a technology-forward mindset and leveraging emerging technologies like artificial intelligence (AI) to drive business growth and innovation.

Adopting a technology-forward mindset means recognizing the potential of digital tools and solutions to transform the way you do business and constantly seeking out new ways to integrate technology into your operations. By embracing technology as a catalyst for growth, you can unlock new opportunities, streamline processes, and ultimately create a more efficient and profitable business.

HERE ARE SOME KEY STRATEGIES FOR EMBRACING technology and harnessing AI as a catalyst for growth:

1. STAY INFORMED ABOUT TECHNOLOGICAL ADVANCEMENTS: To effectively leverage technology, it's essential to stay informed about the latest advancements and trends, particularly in the realm of AI. Subscribe to industry newsletters, follow thought leaders on social media, and attend relevant conferences and webinars. By staying informed, you'll be better positioned to identify emerging technologies that can drive growth and success in your business.

2. DEVELOP A DIGITAL TRANSFORMATION STRATEGY: To successfully integrate AI and other digital technologies into your business, it's essential to have a clear and comprehensive digital transformation strategy in place. This should include a roadmap for integrating AI and other digital tools into your operations, along with clearly defined objectives and success metrics. By having a well-thought-out strategy in place, you can ensure a smooth transition and maximize the return on your technology investments.

. . .

3. Invest in the Right Technology Infrastructure: To harness the full potential of AI and other digital technologies, it's crucial to have the right technology infrastructure in place. This includes investing in cloud-based platforms, data storage solutions, and advanced analytics tools that can support AI-driven innovation. By investing in the right infrastructure, you can ensure that your business is well-equipped to leverage emerging technologies and stay ahead of the competition.

4. Foster a Culture of Innovation and Continuous Learning: To effectively harness AI and other digital technologies, it's essential to foster a culture of innovation and continuous learning within your organization. Encourage your employees to stay informed about the latest technological advancements, experiment with new tools and processes, and embrace the potential of AI to drive growth and success in your business.

5. Collaborate with Tech Partners and Experts: As an entrepreneur, you don't need to navigate the world of AI and digital innovation alone. Seek out partnerships with technology companies, industry experts, and AI solution providers who can help you identify and implement the right technologies for your business. By collaborating with experts, you can gain valuable insights and accelerate the

integration of AI and other digital tools into your operations.

Embracing technology as a catalyst for growth is crucial for entrepreneurial success in the digital age. By staying informed about emerging technologies, developing a clear digital transformation strategy, and fostering a culture of innovation and continuous learning, you can harness the power of AI and other digital innovations to drive growth and success in your business.

The Role of AI in Modern Entrepreneurship: Revolutionizing Business Practices and Unlocking New Opportunities

In the era of digital transformation, artificial intelligence (AI) has emerged as a powerful force shaping modern entrepreneurship. From automating tasks and streamlining processes to enabling data-driven decision-making and personalizing customer experiences, AI is revolutionizing the way businesses operate and compete. In this section titled "The Role of AI in Modern Entrepreneurship: Revolutionizing Business Practices and Unlocking New Opportunities," we will explore the various ways AI is influencing entrepreneurship and how business owners can leverage this technology to drive growth and success.

. . .

1. AUTOMATING BUSINESS PROCESSES: ONE OF THE MOST significant impacts of AI on entrepreneurship is the ability to automate a wide range of business processes. By employing AI-driven tools and solutions, entrepreneurs can automate repetitive and time-consuming tasks, such as data entry, customer service, and inventory management. This not only saves time and resources but also enables entrepreneurs to focus on more strategic aspects of their businesses.

2. ENHANCING CUSTOMER EXPERIENCE: AI IS PLAYING A crucial role in personalizing customer experiences and improving customer satisfaction. With AI-powered tools like chatbots and recommendation engines, businesses can offer personalized product recommendations, targeted marketing campaigns, and 24/7 customer support, leading to increased customer engagement and loyalty.

3. DATA-DRIVEN DECISION-MAKING: ENTREPRENEURS CAN leverage AI-powered analytics tools to gain valuable insights into customer behavior, market trends, and business performance. By analyzing large volumes of data, these tools can help entrepreneurs make more informed decisions about product development, marketing strategies, pricing, and more. This data-driven approach enables entrepreneurs to

adapt more quickly to changing market conditions and stay ahead of the competition.

4. Innovating Products and Services: AI is also enabling entrepreneurs to develop innovative products and services by providing insights into customer preferences, identifying gaps in the market, and accelerating the proto-typing and testing process. By incorporating AI-driven tools and solutions into their product development process, entre-preneurs can bring new products and services to market more quickly and efficiently.

5. Scaling Business Operations: AI-powered tools and solutions can help entrepreneurs scale their businesses by optimizing supply chain management, automating customer acquisition, and improving financial forecasting. By lever-aging AI, entrepreneurs can drive operational efficiencies, reduce costs, and ultimately achieve sustainable growth.

6. Enhancing Competitive Advantage: AI is not only transforming business practices but also leveling the playing field for entrepreneurs. By adopting AI-powered tools and solutions, small businesses can compete more effectively with larger, more established companies. This enables entre-

preneurs to gain a competitive edge in the market and drive long-term success.

AI IS PLAYING A PIVOTAL ROLE IN SHAPING MODERN entrepreneurship by revolutionizing business practices, enhancing customer experiences, and unlocking new opportunities for growth and innovation. By understanding the potential of AI and incorporating this technology into their businesses, entrepreneurs can position themselves for success in the digital age.

FINAL THOUGHTS

As we conclude this chapter, it is evident that artificial intelligence (AI) is revolutionizing the landscape of entrepreneurship and providing businesses with unparalleled opportunities for growth and success. The transformative power of AI lies in its ability to automate processes, enhance customer experiences, enable data-driven decision-making, spur innovation, and level the playing field for small businesses.

In this new era of digital transformation, entrepreneurs who recognize the potential of AI and embrace it as a catalyst for change are more likely to thrive in an increasingly competitive marketplace. By leveraging AI-powered tools and solutions, entrepreneurs can streamline their operations, improve customer satisfaction, and ultimately achieve sustainable growth.

However, adopting AI is not without its challenges. Entrepreneurs must also be mindful of the ethical considerations, data privacy concerns, and workforce implications that come with the integration of AI technologies. By addressing these concerns and fostering a culture of innovation and continuous learning, entrepreneurs can ensure the responsible and effective use of AI in their businesses.

As we move forward, the role of AI in entrepreneurship will continue to evolve and shape the future of business. By staying informed about the latest AI advancements and embracing the potential of this transformative technology, entrepreneurs can unlock new opportunities, drive growth, and ultimately achieve long-term success in the ever-changing world of business.

CHAPTER 2

IDENTIFYING BUSINESS OPPORTUNITIES WITH AI: A NEW FRONTIER FOR ENTREPRENEURS

ARTIFICIAL INTELLIGENCE (AI) IS NO LONGER THE STUFF OF science fiction—it has become an integral part of the modern business landscape, opening up a world of possibilities for entrepreneurs. With AI, businesses can automate processes, analyze vast amounts of data, and even interact with customers in ways that were once unimaginable. For entrepreneurs, recognizing and capitalizing on the potential of AI can lead to the creation of innovative products, services, and business models that can propel their ventures to new heights. In this section, we will explore the ways in which entrepreneurs can identify business opportunities with AI and how this powerful technology can serve as a catalyst for growth and innovation.

One of the first steps in identifying business opportunities with AI is understanding the technology's capabilities and potential applications. This involves familiarizing oneself with the various subfields of AI, such as machine learning, natural language processing, and computer vision, and exploring the ways in which these technologies can be applied to solve real-world problems. By staying informed about the latest advancements in AI, entrepreneurs can identify areas where AI can be leveraged to create innovative solutions that cater to market needs.

Another crucial aspect of identifying business opportunities with AI is analyzing the market and competitive landscape. Entrepreneurs should assess the current state of their industry and identify gaps or inefficiencies that can be addressed using AI. This may involve exploring how AI is being used by competitors, identifying areas where AI can be used to gain a competitive advantage, or finding opportunities to disrupt existing markets with AI-driven solutions.

Additionally, entrepreneurs should consider the potential of AI to enhance their existing products or services. This may involve integrating AI-powered features to improve the user experience, streamline operations, or offer personalized recommendations to customers. By incorporating AI into their offerings, entrepreneurs can stay ahead of the competition and cater to the evolving needs and preferences of their target audience.

Finally, it is essential for entrepreneurs to maintain a future-oriented mindset when identifying business opportunities with AI. As AI continues to evolve and mature, the potential for new and innovative applications will only grow. Entrepreneurs should keep a close eye on emerging trends and technologies in the AI space and consider how these developments might open up new opportunities for their business.

AI presents a wealth of opportunities for entrepreneurs who are willing to embrace this powerful technology and explore its potential to transform their businesses. By staying informed about the latest advancements in AI, analyzing the market landscape, and adopting a future-oriented mindset, entrepreneurs can identify and seize the opportunities that AI has to offer, paving the way for growth, innovation, and long-term success.

RECOGNIZING AI-DRIVEN BUSINESS NICHES: UNLOCKING NEW OPPORTUNITIES FOR ENTREPRENEURS

The rise of artificial intelligence (AI) has led to the emergence of numerous AI-driven business niches, presenting a wealth of opportunities for entrepreneurs who are keen to leverage the power of AI in their ventures. These niches span a wide range of industries and use cases, offering innovative solutions to problems that were once thought to be insurmountable. In this section, we will explore the process of recognizing AI-driven business niches and how entrepreneurs can capitalize on these emerging opportunities to drive growth and success.

One of the key factors in recognizing AI-driven business niches is staying informed about the latest developments and trends in AI technology. This involves keeping up with industry news, attending conferences and workshops, and networking with AI experts and professionals. By staying up-to-date with the AI landscape, entrepreneurs can spot new applications and emerging niches that may be ripe for disruption.

Another important aspect of recognizing AI-driven business niches is understanding the unique problems and pain points that can be addressed using AI technology. Entrepreneurs should engage in market research, customer interviews, and competitor analysis to identify areas where AI can be used to create innovative solutions that cater to unmet needs or improve upon existing offerings. By understanding the specific problems that AI can solve, entrepreneurs can better position their ventures to capitalize on these emerging niches.

Once potential AI-driven business niches have been identified, entrepreneurs should evaluate their feasibility and potential for growth. This involves assessing the market size, barriers to entry, and the competitive landscape. Entrepreneurs should also consider the technical and resource requirements associated with building AI-driven solutions and the potential return on investment (ROI) of pursuing these opportunities.

In addition to recognizing existing AI-driven business niches, entrepreneurs should also be open to the possibility of creating entirely new niches by combining AI with other emerging technologies or applying AI to previously unexplored industries. This may involve thinking outside the box and looking for ways to disrupt traditional markets by offering AI-powered solutions that cater to evolving customer needs and preferences.

Recognizing AI-driven business niches is an essential step for entrepreneurs looking to harness the power of AI in their ventures. By staying informed about the latest developments in AI, understanding the problems that AI can solve, and evaluating the potential for growth and success, entrepreneurs can identify and capitalize on the opportunities presented by these emerging niches, driving innovation and growth in their businesses.

CREATING NEW PRODUCTS OR SERVICES LEVERAGING AI: IGNITING INNOVATION FOR ENTREPRENEURIAL SUCCESS

The integration of artificial intelligence (AI) into the development of new products and services has become increasingly crucial for entrepreneurs seeking to stay competitive and drive innovation in their businesses. By leveraging AI, entrepreneurs can create cutting-edge solutions that cater to evolving customer needs, streamline processes, and ultimately deliver greater value to their target market. In this section, we will discuss the key steps and considerations involved in creating new products or services that harness the power of AI technology.

1. IDENTIFYING OPPORTUNITIES FOR AI INTEGRATION: THE first step in creating AI-powered products or services is to identify areas within your business or industry where AI can have a meaningful impact. This may involve addressing existing pain points, automating repetitive tasks, or providing personalized experiences for your customers. By pinpointing these opportunities, you can better understand the specific use cases for AI within your venture and determine how AI can be used to create innovative solutions that meet your customers' needs.

2. CONDUCTING MARKET RESEARCH: ONCE YOU HAVE identified potential AI integration opportunities, it is essential to conduct thorough market research to understand the competitive landscape, consumer preferences, and any potential barriers to entry. This research will help you refine your AI-powered product or service concept, ensuring that it aligns with your target audience's needs and has a unique selling proposition that sets it apart from competitors.

. . .

3. ASSEMBLING A SKILLED TEAM: BUILDING AI-DRIVEN products or services requires a team with diverse skills and expertise, including data scientists, software developers, and domain experts. Assembling a team with the right mix of skills and experience is critical to the successful development and implementation of your AI-powered solution. This may involve hiring new employees, partnering with AI specialists, or providing training to existing team members.

4. DEVELOPING A MINIMUM VIABLE PRODUCT (MVP): With your team in place and a clear understanding of your AI-powered product or service concept, it's time to develop a minimum viable product (MVP). An MVP is a simplified version of your final product that can be used to test the viability of your concept, gather feedback from potential customers, and iterate on your design. By creating an MVP, you can minimize the time and resources spent on development while maximizing the potential for success.

5. ITERATING AND REFINING YOUR AI SOLUTION: BASED ON the feedback received from your MVP, you'll need to make any necessary adjustments to your AI-powered product or service. This may involve refining the AI algorithms, addressing any technical issues, or making changes to the user interface. By iterating and refining your solution, you

can ensure that it meets the needs of your target audience and delivers the desired value.

6. Launching and Scaling Your AI-Powered Product or Service: Once your AI-powered solution has been refined and tested, it's time to launch it to the market. This may involve a phased rollout, targeted marketing campaigns, or strategic partnerships to gain traction and drive adoption. As your product or service gains momentum, you'll need to focus on scaling your operations, optimizing your AI technology, and continuously improving your offering based on customer feedback and market trends.

Creating new products or services leveraging AI can be a transformative process for entrepreneurs looking to drive innovation and growth in their businesses. By identifying opportunities for AI integration, conducting market research, assembling a skilled team, developing and refining an MVP, and launching and scaling your AI-powered solution, you can harness the power of AI to deliver exceptional value to your customers and stay ahead of the competition.

DISRUPTING TRADITIONAL INDUSTRIES WITH AI SOLUTIONS: THE ENTREPRENEURIAL PATH TO INDUSTRY TRANSFORMATION

In today's rapidly evolving business landscape, artificial intelligence (AI) has emerged as a powerful tool for entrepreneurs seeking to disrupt traditional industries and reshape the way business is conducted. By harnessing AI's capabilities, startups and small businesses can develop innovative solutions that challenge the status quo, drive efficiency, and deliver enhanced value to customers.

The first step in disrupting traditional industries with AI solutions is to pinpoint areas ripe for transformation. This may involve identifying inefficiencies in existing processes, gaps in service offerings, or opportunities to enhance customer experiences. By understanding the specific pain points and challenges within an industry, entrepreneurs can develop targeted AI solutions that address these issues and revolutionize the way business is conducted.

Once potential areas for disruption have been identified, the next step is to develop AI-powered solutions that tackle these challenges head-on. This may involve leveraging machine learning algorithms to optimize processes, natural language processing to improve customer interactions, or computer vision to enhance product offerings. By incorporating AI into your solution, you can create a more efficient, effective, and innovative approach to solving industry-specific problems.

Disrupting traditional industries often requires collaboration with established players who have the resources, networks, and expertise needed to facilitate industry-wide change. By forming strategic partnerships with key stakeholders, entrepreneurs can gain access to valuable resources, expand their market reach, and accelerate the adoption of their AI-powered solutions. These partnerships can be mutually beneficial, as established businesses can also benefit from the innovation and efficiency that AI-driven solutions provide. By embracing AI as a catalyst for disruption, entrepreneurs can pave the way for industry transformation and unlock new opportunities for growth and success.

FINAL THOUGHTS

As we conclude this chapter, it is evident that artificial intelligence holds immense potential for entrepreneurs seeking to innovate, disrupt, and grow their businesses. By understanding the transformative power of AI, entrepreneurs can identify opportunities for its application, develop innovative solutions, and challenge traditional industry norms. AI enables startups and small businesses to optimize their operations, enhance customer experiences, and create more efficient and effective products and services.

Entrepreneurs must cultivate an innovation-focused mindset and embrace technology as a catalyst for growth. By doing so, they can harness the power of AI to identify and seize new opportunities, disrupt traditional industries, and drive success in today's competitive business landscape. This chapter has provided an overview of the potential of AI for startups and small businesses and has highlighted the importance of early AI adoption for entrepreneurs.

As you progress through the book, you will gain deeper insights into the various aspects of implementing AI in your business, from marketing and sales to operations and product development. With the knowledge and guidance provided, you will be well-equipped to embrace the potential of AI and build a successful, AI-powered business. The journey towards AI-driven entrepreneurship begins here, and the opportunities for growth and success are limitless.

CHAPTER 3

AI-POWERED BUSINESS PLANNING AND STRATEGY: AN INTRODUCTION TO DATA-DRIVEN DECISION MAKING FOR ENTREPRENEURS

THE MODERN ENTREPRENEURIAL LANDSCAPE IS INCREASINGLY competitive and complex, requiring business owners to make well-informed decisions and plan strategically to ensure success. With the advent of artificial intelligence, entrepreneurs now have the opportunity to tap into the power of AI to enhance their business planning and strategy development processes. In this section, we will introduce the concept of AI-powered business planning and strategy, exploring how data-driven insights can help entrepreneurs make better decisions, optimize their operations, and gain a competitive edge in the market.

By leveraging AI-powered analytics and forecasting tools, entrepreneurs can access valuable insights derived from large volumes of data, enabling them to make more informed decisions and develop robust strategies. These tools can help business owners identify trends, uncover hidden patterns, and predict future market dynamics, all of which are crucial for developing effective business plans and staying ahead of the competition.

Additionally, AI can help entrepreneurs optimize their marketing and sales strategies by identifying the most effective channels, targeting the right customer segments, and personalizing their messaging. This level of customization and precision can significantly improve the return on investment (ROI) of marketing campaigns and drive sales growth.

AI-powered tools can also enhance strategic decision-making in areas such as supply chain management, financial management, and human resource management. By analyzing data from various sources, AI can help entrepreneurs identify inefficiencies, reduce costs, and streamline processes, leading to improved overall business performance.

In summary, AI-powered business planning and strategy can provide entrepreneurs with the insights and tools they need to navigate the complexities of today's business environment. By embracing data-driven decision making and leveraging the power of AI, entrepreneurs can develop more effective strategies and position their businesses for long-term success. In the following sections, we will delve deeper into the various aspects of AI-powered business planning and strategy, providing practical guidance and examples to help entrepreneurs harness the potential of AI in their businesses.

INCORPORATING AI INTO BUSINESS PLANS: A STRATEGIC APPROACH FOR ENTREPRENEURS

Artificial intelligence (AI) is rapidly transforming the business landscape, making it crucial for entrepreneurs to consider incorporating AI into their business plans. Doing so allows them to harness the technology's potential for driving growth and improving operational efficiency. In this section, we outline the key steps and considerations for integrating AI into business plans, offering a roadmap for entrepreneurs as they embrace this revolutionary technology.

The first step in incorporating AI into a business plan is identifying the areas where AI can have the most significant impact on your business. This may involve automating repetitive tasks, enhancing customer service, streamlining decision-making processes, or optimizing supply chain management. Evaluating your current processes and operations can help pinpoint opportunities for AI implementation. Once you have identified these opportunities, it is essential to define your objectives clearly. Establishing specific, measurable, achievable, relevant, and time-bound (SMART) goals will help maintain focus and measure the progress and success of your AI initiatives.

As you move forward, research and evaluate various AI solutions to find the ones that best align with your goals and business needs. Factors such as cost, scalability, ease of integration, and support should be considered when making your decision. After selecting the appropriate AI solutions, create a detailed implementation plan outlining the steps and resources required to integrate AI into your business. This plan should include timelines, budget allocations, personnel requirements, and any necessary training or upskilling initiatives.

Lastly, continually monitor and evaluate the progress of your AI integration to ensure that your objectives are being met and to make any necessary adjustments along the way. By following this strategic approach, entrepreneurs can successfully integrate AI into their business plans and capitalize on the immense potential that AI has to offer.

ADAPTING TO MARKET CHANGES WITH AI INSIGHTS: STAYING AHEAD OF THE CURVE

In today's fast-paced business environment, the ability to adapt to market changes quickly is crucial for entrepreneurial success. AI can play a vital role in providing timely insights and helping businesses stay ahead of the curve. In this section, we discuss how entrepreneurs can leverage AI to better understand market shifts and adjust their strategies accordingly.

AI-powered analytics tools can collect, analyze, and interpret vast amounts of data from various sources, such as customer interactions, social media, competitor activities, and industry trends. By processing this data in real-time, AI algorithms can uncover hidden patterns and generate actionable insights, enabling entrepreneurs to make data-driven decisions with greater confidence.

One of the primary benefits of using AI to analyze market changes is the ability to identify emerging trends and consumer preferences. By continually monitoring customer behavior and feedback, AI systems can help businesses identify new opportunities, tailor their product offerings, and target their marketing efforts more effectively. This can result in improved customer satisfaction, increased sales, and a more robust market position.

Additionally, AI can provide valuable insights into competitor activities and strategies, allowing businesses to adapt and remain competitive. By monitoring and analyzing competitor pricing, promotions, and product launches, AI can help entrepreneurs identify potential threats and opportunities, enabling them to make informed strategic decisions.

Moreover, AI can assist in identifying operational inefficiencies and areas for improvement within a business. By analyzing internal data, AI-powered systems can pinpoint bottlenecks, redundancies, and other issues that may be impacting performance. This information can then be used to optimize processes, reduce costs, and enhance overall efficiency.

The ability to adapt to market changes is vital for entrepreneurial success, and AI can play a crucial role in providing the insights needed to stay ahead of the curve. By harnessing the power of AI, entrepreneurs can make more informed decisions, improve their operations, and ultimately achieve greater success in an ever-changing business landscape.

FINAL THOUGHTS

As we conclude this chapter, it is clear that AI has the potential to revolutionize the way entrepreneurs approach business planning and strategy. From incorporating AI into business plans to adapting to market changes with AI insights, the technology's applications are vast and diverse, offering a wealth of opportunities for businesses of all sizes.

To remain competitive in the modern business world, entrepreneurs must embrace AI as a valuable tool for growth and success. By leveraging AI-powered analytics, businesses can make more informed decisions, optimize their operations, and better understand their customers and competitors. This will enable entrepreneurs to create and implement more effective strategies, ultimately leading to increased growth, profitability, and sustainability.

It is essential, however, for entrepreneurs to approach AI adoption with a proactive and open-minded attitude. As the technology continues to evolve, businesses must remain adaptable and committed to learning and implementing new AI capabilities. By fostering a culture of innovation and embracing change, entrepreneurs can harness the full potential of AI and stay ahead of the curve in today's rapidly shifting business landscape.

Chapter 4

Navigating the Funding Landscape for AI-Driven Startups

Embarking on the journey of entrepreneurship with an AI-driven startup can be both exhilarating and challenging. One of the most critical aspects of establishing a successful business is securing the necessary funding and investment to fuel growth and innovation. In this chapter, we will explore the unique funding landscape for AI-driven startups and provide insights and guidance on how entrepreneurs can attract investors and secure the financial support needed to bring their AI-powered ventures to life.

As AI continues to transform industries and redefine the way businesses operate, there is a growing demand for AI-driven solutions, making the market ripe for innovative startups. Investors are increasingly eager to back promising AI ventures, recognizing the potential for significant returns on their investments. However, this also means that competition for funding can be fierce, and entrepreneurs must effectively communicate the value of their AI-driven solutions and demonstrate a clear path to success.

In the following sections, we will delve into various funding sources, from angel investors and venture capital firms to government grants and crowdfunding platforms. We will discuss how to craft a compelling pitch, showcase the potential of your AI-driven product or service, and build strong relationships with potential investors. By understanding the funding landscape and employing strategic approaches to securing investment, entrepreneurs can create a solid foundation for their AI-driven startups, setting the stage for long-term growth and success.

THE INVESTMENT LANDSCAPE FOR AI-DRIVEN BUSINESSES

The rapid growth and expansion of artificial intelligence have led to an increasingly competitive investment landscape for AI-driven businesses. As more and more entrepreneurs recognize the transformative potential of AI, investors are becoming keenly interested in backing startups that can leverage this technology to disrupt industries and create lasting value. In this section, we will examine the various types of investors and funding sources available to AI-driven businesses, providing insights on how to navigate this complex landscape and secure the necessary resources to fuel growth.

Angel investors, often successful entrepreneurs themselves, are known for providing early-stage financial support and guidance to startups. These individuals can offer not only funding but also valuable industry connections and mentorship. Targeting angel investors with a background in AI or a track record of backing AI-driven businesses can increase your chances of securing their support.

Venture capital (VC) firms are another key player in the investment landscape for AI-driven businesses. VCs typically invest in startups with high growth potential in exchange for equity. They tend to be more risk-tolerant than other investors, and many VC firms have dedicated AI-focused funds or investment strategies. To attract VC funding, entrepreneurs must demonstrate a strong business model, a clear competitive advantage, and the potential for significant returns on investment.

In addition to angel investors and VC firms, AI-driven businesses can also explore other funding sources such as government grants, accelerators, and incubators. These programs often provide financial support, mentorship, and resources to help startups develop and refine their products and services. Some programs specifically target AI-driven businesses, while others focus on broader technology sectors or industries ripe for disruption.

Finally, crowdfunding platforms have emerged as a popular alternative to traditional funding sources, enabling entrepreneurs to raise capital directly from the public. By showcasing their AI-driven products or services on platforms like Kickstarter or Indiegogo, startups can generate buzz, validate market demand, and secure funding from numerous individual backers.

Navigating the investment landscape for AI-driven businesses requires a thorough understanding of the various funding sources and a tailored approach to securing support. By identifying the right investors and funding opportunities, entrepreneurs can access the resources needed to build, grow, and scale their AI-driven ventures.

CRAFTING A COMPELLING PITCH FOR AI-FOCUSED INVESTORS

Successfully securing funding for your AI-driven startup depends not only on the strength of your business idea but also on your ability to communicate its potential to investors. In this section, we will outline key strategies for crafting a compelling pitch that showcases the value of your AI-driven solution and captures the attention of AI-focused investors.

1. CLEARLY ARTICULATE THE PROBLEM AND SOLUTION: START by presenting the problem your AI-driven product or service aims to solve. Be specific about the market gap and the pain points experienced by your target customers. Then, succinctly explain how your AI-powered solution addresses

these issues, emphasizing the benefits and competitive advantages it offers.

2. SHOWCASE YOUR AI EXPERTISE: AI-FOCUSED INVESTORS will want to see that you have a deep understanding of the technology and its applications. Demonstrate your knowledge of AI by discussing the algorithms, models, or techniques that underpin your solution. Highlight any unique or proprietary aspects of your AI technology that set it apart from competitors.

3. QUANTIFY THE MARKET OPPORTUNITY: INVESTORS NEED to understand the potential returns on their investment, so it's essential to provide data-driven insights into the size of the market opportunity. Use market research, industry reports, and other sources to estimate the addressable market and the potential revenue for your AI-driven solution. Be sure to emphasize the scalability of your business model and the potential for global expansion.

4. PRESENT YOUR BUSINESS MODEL AND GO-TO-MARKET strategy: Clearly outline your revenue streams, pricing strategy, sales channels, and customer acquisition plans. Explain how your AI-driven solution will be positioned in the market, who your target customers are, and how you will

reach and engage them. Be prepared to discuss the potential for strategic partnerships or collaborations that could help drive adoption of your AI-powered offering.

5. DEMONSTRATE TRACTION AND PROGRESS: IF YOU'VE already achieved milestones, such as a successful product launch, customer traction, or early-stage funding, be sure to highlight these achievements. Share any positive feedback, testimonials, or case studies that demonstrate the real-world impact of your AI-driven solution.

6. INTRODUCE YOUR TEAM: INVESTORS OFTEN PLACE A premium on the quality of the founding team, so take the time to introduce your key team members and their relevant expertise. Highlight any previous successes or experiences that demonstrate your ability to execute on your vision.

7. ADDRESS POTENTIAL RISKS AND CHALLENGES: BE transparent about the risks and challenges your AI-driven startup may face, such as regulatory hurdles, data privacy concerns, or technical barriers. Show that you have considered these issues and have a plan in place to mitigate and manage them.

. . .

BY FOLLOWING THESE GUIDELINES AND TAILORING YOUR pitch to the interests and priorities of AI-focused investors, you can increase your chances of securing the funding and support needed to bring your AI-driven business to life.

NAVIGATING FUNDING OPTIONS FOR AI INTEGRATION AND DEVELOPMENT

As an entrepreneur venturing into the world of AI, securing the necessary funding can be a crucial step towards achieving your goals. Understanding the various funding options available to you is essential for a smooth journey in integrating AI into your business or developing AI-driven solutions.

Initially, self-funding or bootstrapping may be the most viable option, especially for smaller-scale AI projects. This approach involves using personal savings, tapping into resources from friends and family, or reinvesting revenue from your existing business. Bootstrapping can be a great way to maintain control over your business and minimize the need for external financing, but it may limit your capacity for rapid growth.

It's also worth exploring grants and government programs, as many governments and organizations recognize the importance of AI in driving innovation and economic growth. These programs may provide financial support, resources, and networking opportunities to entrepreneurs working on AI projects.

Additionally, there are various forms of private invest-ment, such as angel investors, venture capital firms, and corporate partnerships. These investors may be particularly interested in AI-driven startups due to the high growth potential in this sector. When seeking funding from private investors, it's crucial to craft a compelling pitch and demon-strate how AI can provide a competitive edge for your business.

Navigating the funding landscape for AI integration and development requires thorough research, persistence, and a clear understanding of your business's unique value proposi-tion. By exploring a range of financing options, you can secure the necessary resources to drive your AI-driven busi-ness towards success.

FINAL THOUGHTS

As we reach the conclusion of this chapter, it is evident that AI has the potential to revolutionize startups and small busi-nesses. From identifying business opportunities to creating innovative products and services, AI can be a game-changer for entrepreneurs who are willing to embrace this powerful technology.

By understanding the investment landscape, crafting compelling pitches, and navigating various funding options, entrepreneurs can secure the resources they need to build and grow their AI-driven ventures. Moreover, leveraging AI for business planning and strategy allows startups to stay ahead of market trends and adapt to changes with agility and precision.

As an entrepreneur, it's essential to maintain an innovation-focused mindset and recognize the opportunities that AI presents. By doing so, you can harness the power of artificial intelligence to propel your business towards growth and success. With determination, adaptability, and a clear vision, you can lead the way in the AI-driven future of entrepreneurship.

Chapter 5

Building an AI-Driven Team: Laying the Foundation for Success

In the dynamic world of AI-driven businesses, assembling the right team is a critical factor in ensuring long-term success. An AI-driven team consists of diverse skill sets, innovative thinking, and a deep understanding of the technology that underpins artificial intelligence. In this chapter, we will explore the importance of building a team that can effectively harness the power of AI to drive your startup or small business towards growth and success. By understanding the key roles, fostering a culture of innovation, and nurturing talent, you can create a team that is well-equipped to navigate the complexities of the AI landscape and make a significant impact in your industry.

Attracting and Retaining AI Talent: Winning the War for Top Talent

The rapid advancement of AI has led to an increasing demand for skilled professionals in the field, making the competition for talent fiercer than ever. To attract and retain top AI talent for your startup or small business, it is essential to create an environment that fosters learning, innovation, and growth. Offering competitive compensation packages, flexible work arrangements, and opportunities for personal and professional development will help draw in the best and brightest minds in AI.

Additionally, focus on creating a culture of collaboration and inclusivity where team members feel valued and can contribute meaningfully to the company's goals. This includes providing access to cutting-edge tools and technology, encouraging continuous learning, and promoting a healthy work-life balance. By creating a supportive and stimulating environment, you will not only attract top AI talent but also inspire their loyalty and commitment, ensuring that your business remains at the forefront of the AI revolution.

Collaborating with AI Experts and Researchers: Forging Synergistic Partnerships

In today's fast-paced AI landscape, collaboration with experts and researchers in the field can greatly enhance your business's growth and innovation potential. Establishing partnerships with academic institutions, research organizations, and industry leaders can provide invaluable insights, access to cutting-edge technology, and networking opportunities. These collaborations can help your business stay ahead of the curve, refine its AI strategy, and develop groundbreaking products or services.

To forge successful partnerships, consider participating in industry conferences, workshops, and seminars where you can connect with AI experts and researchers. Building relationships with these individuals can lead to mutually beneficial collaborations, such as joint research projects, mentorship opportunities, or even talent acquisition. Additionally, consider sponsoring or hosting hackathons, meetups, and other community events that can showcase your company's commitment to innovation and attract AI professionals. By actively engaging with the AI community and fostering a spirit of collaboration, you can position your business as a key player in the industry and tap into the wealth of knowledge and expertise that AI experts and researchers have to offer.

BALANCING HUMAN AND AI-DRIVEN ROLES IN THE ORGANIZATION: THE ART OF SYNERGY AND EFFICIENCY

As AI technologies continue to advance and reshape the business landscape, entrepreneurs must find the right balance between human and AI-driven roles within their organizations. This equilibrium is critical for creating an efficient and innovative work environment that maximizes the potential of both human and artificial intelligence.

To achieve this balance, entrepreneurs should begin by identifying tasks and processes that can be effectively automated or augmented by AI. This might include data analysis, customer support, or inventory management, among others. By automating repetitive and time-consuming tasks, businesses can free up human resources to focus on more strategic, creative, and relationship-driven aspects of their roles.

Next, entrepreneurs should invest in upskilling and reskilling their workforce to help them adapt to the changing work environment. Providing training and development programs in AI-related fields can empower employees to work alongside AI-driven tools, fostering a collaborative and symbiotic relationship. This approach will ensure that your team remains competitive and relevant in the AI age.

Additionally, creating a culture of open communication and transparency around AI implementation is crucial. Encourage dialogue between employees and AI experts to address concerns, gather feedback, and create a shared understanding of the benefits and limitations of AI technologies. By acknowledging the importance of both human and AI-driven roles, you can build a resilient and agile organization that is well-prepared for the future of work.

FINAL THOUGHTS

As we conclude this chapter on building an AI-driven team, it is essential to recognize the transformative potential that AI holds for businesses of all sizes. By attracting and retaining top AI talent, fostering collaboration with AI experts and researchers, and striking the right balance between human and AI-driven roles, entrepreneurs can harness the power of artificial intelligence to drive innovation, efficiency, and growth.

As an entrepreneur, it is crucial to stay ahead of the curve by adopting a proactive approach towards AI integration. This involves staying informed about the latest advancements in AI, investing in employee training, and cultivating a culture of openness and adaptability. By embracing the AI-driven future, you will position your business for long-term success and establish yourself as a leader in your industry.

Remember that the journey of integrating AI into your business is an ongoing process. As new technologies emerge and the AI landscape evolves, there will be continuous opportunities to adapt and improve. Stay curious, be open to change, and remember that the synergistic partnership between human and artificial intelligence is the key to unlocking the full potential of AI for your business.

CHAPTER 6

LEVERAGING AI FOR MARKET RESEARCH AND CUSTOMER INSIGHTS

THE DAWN OF THE AI ERA HAS REVOLUTIONIZED THE WAY businesses approach market research and customer insights. With a wealth of data at our fingertips, the potential to gain a deeper understanding of consumer behavior, preferences, and trends has never been greater. In this chapter, we will explore how entrepreneurs can harness the power of artificial intelligence to make informed decisions and drive strategic growth.

From natural language processing to machine learning algorithms, AI-driven market research tools are rapidly transforming the way businesses analyze data and gain insights into customer behavior. These advanced technologies enable entrepreneurs to identify emerging trends, uncover hidden patterns, and better understand their target audience, all of which are critical for crafting effective marketing strategies and delivering exceptional customer experiences.

By embracing AI-driven market research and customer insights, entrepreneurs can unlock new opportunities for innovation, streamline operations, and ultimately, achieve a competitive advantage in an increasingly data-driven world.

UTILIZING AI FOR COMPREHENSIVE MARKET ANALYSIS

The business landscape is constantly shifting, making it essential for entrepreneurs to stay ahead of the curve. Comprehensive market analysis is crucial for identifying potential opportunities and threats, and artificial intelligence is transforming this process by providing powerful new tools and insights. In this section, we will discuss how AI can enhance market analysis, enabling entrepreneurs to make more informed decisions and drive their businesses forward.

Traditional market analysis methods, such as focus groups and surveys, can be time-consuming, expensive, and prone to human error. AI-powered tools, on the other hand, can analyze vast amounts of data in real-time, uncovering trends and patterns that might have gone unnoticed. Machine learning algorithms and natural language processing enable businesses to comb through social media feeds, news articles, and customer reviews, providing a wealth of information about customer preferences, competitor strategies, and market dynamics.

AI-driven market analysis also has the potential to identify emerging trends and technologies, allowing entrepreneurs to anticipate changes in consumer demand and adjust their strategies accordingly. Furthermore, these advanced tools can help businesses identify gaps in the market, creating opportunities for innovative new products and services.

By incorporating AI into their market analysis process, entrepreneurs can gain a deeper understanding of their industry, customers, and competitors, ultimately empowering them to make data-driven decisions and achieve long-term success in the ever-evolving business world.

GAINING CUSTOMER INSIGHTS THROUGH AI-DRIVEN ANALYTICS

Understanding customers is the key to any business's success, and AI-driven analytics provides a powerful means to access critical insights about their preferences, behaviors, and needs. In this section, we will explore how entrepreneurs can leverage AI-driven analytics to gain valuable customer insights and tailor their products, services, and marketing strategies to meet evolving consumer demands.

AI-powered analytics tools can process vast amounts of customer data from various sources, such as transaction records, website interactions, and social media activity. Machine learning algorithms can identify patterns and trends, revealing valuable information about customer preferences, needs, and pain points. These insights enable businesses to make informed decisions about product development, pricing strategies, and promotional campaigns, ultimately driving customer satisfaction and loyalty.

Sentiment analysis, a subset of natural language processing, can help businesses gauge customer sentiment by analyzing the language used in social media posts, reviews, and other online interactions. This enables entrepreneurs to identify areas where their offerings may be falling short and implement improvements to address customer concerns.

Moreover, AI-driven analytics can help businesses segment their customer base and create personalized marketing campaigns that resonate with specific target groups. By understanding the unique preferences of various customer segments, entrepreneurs can optimize their marketing efforts and deliver more relevant, engaging content that drives conversions and fosters long-term customer relationships.

By embracing AI-driven analytics, entrepreneurs can gain a deeper understanding of their customers, allowing them to create products, services, and experiences that resonate with their audience and drive business growth.

Identifying Untapped Market Segments with AI

Uncovering new market segments is a critical component of a successful growth strategy for any entrepreneur. AI-powered tools and techniques can help entrepreneurs identify untapped market segments and capitalize on emerging opportunities, enabling them to stay ahead of the competition and drive innovation in their industries. In this section, we will explore the potential of AI in identifying untapped market segments and providing valuable insights for expansion and growth.

AI-powered market research tools can analyze vast amounts of data from various sources, such as consumer purchasing patterns, online reviews, and social media activity. By applying machine learning algorithms and natural language processing techniques, these tools can detect trends, preferences, and unmet needs among consumers. This enables entrepreneurs to spot underserved market segments that they can target with tailored products, services, or marketing strategies.

Predictive analytics is another powerful application of AI that can help entrepreneurs identify potential market opportunities. By leveraging historical data and machine learning models, predictive analytics tools can forecast future trends, enabling businesses to anticipate shifts in consumer behavior or preferences. This forward-looking perspective empowers entrepreneurs to proactively develop new products, services, or campaigns that cater to emerging market segments before competitors can capitalize on them.

Furthermore, AI-driven customer segmentation can help businesses identify niche markets within their existing customer base. By clustering customers based on similar preferences or behaviors, entrepreneurs can tailor their offerings to cater to these distinct groups, unlocking new revenue streams and fostering customer loyalty.

AI offers entrepreneurs a wealth of opportunities to identify untapped market segments and capitalize on emerging trends. By embracing AI-driven tools and techniques, entrepreneurs can innovate and expand their businesses, securing their position as leaders in their respective industries.

FINAL THOUGHTS

As we conclude this chapter, it is clear that AI-driven market research and customer insights play a significant role in empowering entrepreneurs to make informed decisions and stay competitive in today's fast-paced business landscape. The ability to harness AI for comprehensive market analysis, gaining customer insights through analytics, and identifying untapped market segments offers businesses an unprecedented edge in identifying opportunities and driving growth.

Entrepreneurs should invest in developing a strong understanding of AI technologies and how they can be leveraged for market research and customer analysis. By doing so, they can build a solid foundation for implementing AI-powered tools and strategies that will enable them to stay ahead of the competition and continually adapt to the evolving needs of their customers.

Furthermore, entrepreneurs must remain open to embracing new technologies and methods as they emerge, ensuring that their businesses continue to benefit from the latest AI advancements. By staying at the forefront of AI innovation, entrepreneurs can ensure that they are prepared to seize opportunities and drive success in their respective industries.

In summary, this chapter has highlighted the immense potential of AI in transforming market research and customer insights, ultimately empowering entrepreneurs to make data-driven decisions and fuel their businesses' growth. By embracing AI-driven tools and techniques, entrepreneurs can position themselves as industry leaders and capitalize on the opportunities presented by this powerful technology.

Chapter 7

AI-Enhanced Productivity and Time Management for Entrepreneurs

In today's fast-paced business environment, entrepreneurs face constant challenges and demands on their time. As they strive to drive growth, innovate, and stay ahead of the competition, effective productivity and time management become crucial elements for success. In this chapter, we will explore the exciting potential of artificial intelligence (AI) in enhancing productivity and optimizing time management for entrepreneurs.

AI has the power to revolutionize the way entrepreneurs work, enabling them to focus on high-value tasks while automating routine and time-consuming processes. From smart scheduling and prioritization to intelligent delegation and collaboration, AI-driven tools can help entrepreneurs streamline their work, manage their time more effectively, and make better decisions.

As we delve into the various AI applications in productivity and time management, we will discuss the potential benefits and best practices for implementing these technologies in your business. We will also highlight real-life examples of AI-driven solutions that have successfully transformed the way entrepreneurs manage their time and achieve their goals.

Embrace the transformative power of AI and discover how it can revolutionize the way you work, freeing up valuable time and resources to focus on what truly matters: driving the success of your business.

Automating Administrative Tasks for Time Savings with AI

One of the most significant benefits of AI for entrepreneurs lies in its ability to automate administrative tasks, freeing up time and energy for more strategic and creative endeavors. Many routine activities, such as data entry, scheduling, and bookkeeping, can consume a significant portion of an entrepreneur's day, leaving little time for other priorities. By leveraging AI-driven solutions, entrepreneurs can offload these time-consuming tasks and focus on driving their businesses forward.

AI-powered tools like virtual assistants can help manage emails, appointments, and reminders, ensuring that entrepreneurs never miss an important meeting or deadline. Meanwhile, AI-driven data entry and bookkeeping solutions can process and analyze financial transactions, invoices, and other documents with speed and accuracy, minimizing errors and providing valuable insights into business performance.

Furthermore, AI can help automate customer support through chatbots, which can handle inquiries and provide instant responses, ensuring that customers receive prompt assistance without the need for constant human intervention. This not only saves time for entrepreneurs but also enhances the customer experience and helps build brand loyalty.

In summary, by automating administrative tasks with AI, entrepreneurs can save significant time and effort, allowing them to concentrate on high-value tasks such as innovation, strategic planning, and relationship-building. Embracing AI-driven automation is a smart investment that can lead to increased productivity, efficiency, and ultimately, business success.

PRIORITIZING TASKS AND GOALS WITH AI-DRIVEN INSIGHTS

One of the most critical skills for entrepreneurs is the ability to prioritize tasks and goals effectively. With limited time and resources, it's crucial to focus on the activities that will deliver the most significant impact on business growth. AI-driven insights can help entrepreneurs make more informed decisions about where to invest their time and energy, ensuring that their efforts are aligned with their strategic objectives.

AI-powered analytics tools can process vast amounts of data and identify patterns, trends, and correlations that may not be readily apparent to human observers. By analyzing factors such as customer preferences, market trends, and competitor performance, these tools can provide valuable insights into which products, services, or marketing strategies are likely to generate the most significant returns on investment.

In addition to helping entrepreneurs prioritize their strategic goals, AI can also assist in managing daily tasks and activities. AI-driven project management and time tracking tools can analyze historical performance data to determine which tasks typically take the longest, which are the most critical, and which are the most prone to delays or bottlenecks. With this information, entrepreneurs can create more efficient workflows, delegate tasks more effectively, and ensure that their teams are focused on the most impactful activities.

AI-driven insights can play a vital role in helping entrepreneurs prioritize tasks and goals, both in the short term and the long term. By leveraging the power of AI, entrepreneurs can make better-informed decisions, optimize their time and resources, and ultimately drive greater success for their businesses.

ENHANCING PERSONAL PRODUCTIVITY WITH AI-POWERED TOOLS

In today's fast-paced business environment, entrepreneurs often find themselves juggling multiple tasks and responsibilities. To stay competitive, it's essential to find ways to boost personal productivity and make the most of each day. AI-powered tools offer a wide range of capabilities that can help entrepreneurs become more efficient, organized, and focused, ultimately increasing their productivity and effectiveness.

One of the primary benefits of AI-powered tools is their ability to automate repetitive tasks, freeing up valuable time for more strategic and creative pursuits. For example, AI-driven personal assistants can help manage schedules, send reminders, and even draft emails or reports, allowing entrepreneurs to focus on higher-level tasks that require their unique expertise and insights.

AI can also improve decision-making by providing real-time data and insights that help entrepreneurs stay informed and make better choices. For instance, AI-driven analytics tools can help monitor industry trends, track competitor activity, and analyze customer behavior, enabling entrepreneurs to make data-driven decisions that are more likely to lead to success.

Furthermore, AI-powered tools can enhance personal productivity by streamlining communication and collaboration. AI-driven chatbots and virtual assistants can help manage and prioritize incoming messages, making it easier for entrepreneurs to stay on top of essential communications without becoming overwhelmed. Additionally, AI can assist in organizing and searching documents, notes, and files, reducing the time spent searching for critical information.

In summary, AI-powered tools can have a significant impact on an entrepreneur's personal productivity by automating routine tasks, providing real-time insights, and streamlining communication and collaboration. By leveraging the power of AI, entrepreneurs can work more efficiently and effectively, allowing them to dedicate more time and energy to growing their businesses.

FINAL THOUGHTS

As we've explored throughout this chapter, AI holds tremendous promise for entrepreneurs seeking to boost their productivity and optimize their time management. By automating administrative tasks, prioritizing goals with data-driven insights, and leveraging AI-powered tools for personal productivity, entrepreneurs can unlock new levels of efficiency and effectiveness in their daily routines.

While AI may seem like a complex and daunting technology, it's essential to remember that many AI-powered tools are designed with user-friendliness in mind. These tools are accessible to entrepreneurs from diverse backgrounds and industries, making it easier than ever to integrate AI into various aspects of business operations.

As an entrepreneur, embracing AI-driven solutions can help you stay ahead of the curve and remain competitive in an increasingly technology-driven world. By understanding the potential of AI and incorporating it into your business strategies, you can capitalize on the benefits this powerful technology offers to drive growth and success for your enterprise.

In the chapters to follow, we will delve deeper into more specific areas where AI can have a transformative impact on your business. By implementing these cutting-edge technologies, you'll be well on your way to harnessing the full potential of AI and positioning your business for long-term success.

CHAPTER 8

NAVIGATING THE AI ECOSYSTEM FOR NETWORKING AND COLLABORATION

As an entrepreneur, you likely understand the importance of networking and collaboration to the success of your business. As you venture into the realm of AI-driven solutions, the value of engaging with others in the AI ecosystem becomes even more crucial. This chapter will explore the significance of networking and collaboration in the AI ecosystem, highlighting the key players, opportunities, and best practices for building strong relationships within this dynamic field.

The AI ecosystem is vast and diverse, encompassing everything from AI startups and technology giants to research institutions and independent developers. Navigating this complex landscape can be challenging, but it's essential for entrepreneurs seeking to capitalize on the potential of AI for their businesses. By forging connections with the right partners, you can not only accelerate the development and adoption of AI solutions but also ensure that you remain informed about the latest trends and advancements in the field.

In the sections that follow, we'll provide you with practical strategies for building a robust network within the AI ecosystem. We'll discuss the importance of attending AI-focused events, participating in online communities, and collaborating with AI researchers and developers. By engaging with the AI community, you'll gain access to a wealth of resources, expertise, and opportunities that can propel your business to new heights.

ENGAGING WITH AI-FOCUSED COMMUNITIES AND EVENTS: BUILDING A STRONG NETWORK FOR SUCCESS

One of the most effective ways to immerse yourself in the AI ecosystem is by engaging with AI-focused communities and attending relevant events. These platforms provide invaluable opportunities to network with like-minded individuals, learn from experts, and discover potential partnerships. In this section, we'll explore the benefits of participating in AI-focused communities and events and offer tips for making the most of these experiences.

AI-focused communities can take many forms, including online forums, social media groups, and local meetups. These platforms provide a space for individuals with a shared interest in AI to exchange ideas, discuss challenges, and share resources. By joining and actively participating in these communities, you can not only expand your knowledge of AI technologies and applications but also build connections with other entrepreneurs, developers, and researchers who share your passion for AI-driven innovation.

Attending AI-focused events such as conferences, workshops, and hackathons can also be an invaluable networking opportunity. These events often feature presentations from leading experts in the field, offering a wealth of insights into cutting-edge AI research and applications. In addition, attending such events can help you identify potential partners, investors, and collaborators, all of whom could play a crucial role in the growth and success of your AI-driven business.

To make the most of these networking opportunities, it's essential to approach them with a clear goal in mind. Consider what you hope to achieve through your engagement with the AI community, whether it's identifying potential collaborators, staying up to date with industry trends, or gaining insights to help shape your business strategy. By being proactive and strategic in your approach, you can leverage the power of networking and collaboration to drive your AI-driven business forward.

Partnering with AI Startups, Research Organizations, and Industry Leaders: Collaborate to Innovate

In the rapidly evolving AI landscape, partnering with startups, research organizations, and industry leaders can provide a significant competitive advantage for your business. These collaborations can help you access cutting-edge technology, tap into specialized expertise, and accelerate the development of your AI-driven products and services. In this section, we'll discuss the benefits of such partnerships and offer guidance on identifying the right collaborators for your business.

Partnering with AI startups can provide access to innovative technologies that might be the perfect fit for your business needs. These young companies are often at the forefront of the latest AI developments, and collaborating with them can help you stay ahead of the curve in your industry. Moreover, partnering with startups can lead to a mutually beneficial relationship, as they can benefit from your industry experience and customer base, while you can leverage their technical expertise and innovative solutions.

Research organizations, such as universities and research institutes, are another valuable source of AI knowledge and expertise. By collaborating with these organizations, you can tap into a wealth of cutting-edge research and access highly skilled researchers who can contribute to your AI projects. Partnerships with research organizations can take various forms, including joint research projects, technology licensing, or even hiring researchers as consultants or advisors.

Industry leaders, on the other hand, can offer a wealth of experience in implementing AI solutions at scale. By partnering with these established players, you can learn from their successes and failures and incorporate best practices into your own AI-driven business. In addition, partnering with industry leaders can provide opportunities for co-development and co-marketing of AI solutions, allowing you to benefit from their established market presence and customer base.

When seeking potential partners, it's crucial to consider factors such as their technical expertise, industry experience, and alignment with your business goals. By carefully selecting your collaborators and fostering strong partnerships, you can unlock the full potential of AI for your business and drive innovation in your industry.

COLLABORATING ON AI-DRIVEN PROJECTS FOR MUTUAL GROWTH: SYNERGY IN ACTION

Collaborating on AI-driven projects can significantly contribute to the growth and success of all parties involved. By combining resources, knowledge, and expertise, businesses can develop innovative solutions and create a win-win situation that benefits everyone. In this section, we will discuss the advantages of collaborative projects, and how entrepreneurs can ensure the success of these collaborations for mutual growth.

Collaborative AI-driven projects can lead to several benefits, including faster development cycles, reduced costs, and increased innovation. By pooling resources, businesses can share the financial burden of AI projects, while simultaneously gaining access to a diverse range of skills and expertise. This diverse talent pool can help identify creative solutions and bring fresh perspectives to the table, ultimately leading to more innovative products and services.

Furthermore, collaboration on AI projects can help businesses expand their network, build brand awareness, and enter new markets. By working together, businesses can leverage the established reputation and customer base of their partners, making it easier to penetrate new markets and gain credibility within the industry. Collaborative projects can also lead to cross-promotional opportunities, enabling businesses to reach a wider audience and attract new customers.

To ensure the success of collaborative AI-driven projects, it's essential to establish clear goals, roles, and responsibilities from the outset. All parties involved should have a shared understanding of the project's objectives and how their contributions will align with these goals. Communication is critical – regular updates and open dialogue can help prevent misunderstandings and ensure that everyone is working towards the same end.

Finally, it's essential to carefully consider the compatibility of potential partners. Successful collaborations require trust, a shared vision, and complementary skills and expertise. By vetting potential partners and ensuring alignment in terms of values, objectives, and capabilities, businesses can foster strong relationships that lead to successful AI-driven projects and mutual growth.

FINAL THOUGHTS

The AI ecosystem presents a wealth of opportunities for entrepreneurs to expand their networks, forge strong partnerships, and collaborate on groundbreaking projects. By engaging with AI-focused communities, attending industry events, and connecting with leading organizations and startups, entrepreneurs can stay informed about the latest trends, share knowledge, and find like-minded individuals to work with.

Partnering with other businesses, research organizations, and industry leaders can lead to collaborative AI-driven projects that fuel mutual growth and success. These partnerships not only result in innovative products and services but also help businesses expand their reach, build brand awareness, and establish a strong presence in the industry. By pooling resources, sharing expertise, and combining strengths, businesses can maximize the potential of AI technology and create a lasting impact.

As an entrepreneur in the AI space, it's essential to prioritize networking and collaboration as a vital part of your business strategy. By embracing the power of collaboration, you can tap into the collective intelligence of the AI ecosystem and unlock new opportunities for your business. As the world of AI continues to evolve, staying connected and fostering strong relationships will be key to staying competitive and driving success in this rapidly changing landscape.

CHAPTER 9

LAYING THE FOUNDATION FOR MEASURING AI-DRIVEN SUCCESS

AS AN ENTREPRENEUR VENTURING INTO THE REALM OF artificial intelligence, it's essential to understand the importance of measuring and tracking the success of your AI-driven initiatives. In this chapter, we will discuss the best practices for evaluating the impact of AI on your business, identifying key performance indicators (KPIs), and utilizing data-driven insights to optimize your operations, products, and services. By mastering the art of measuring AI success, you can make informed decisions, drive continuous improvement, and ultimately, gain a competitive edge in today's fast-paced business landscape.

ESTABLISHING CLEAR SUCCESS METRICS FOR AI IMPLEMENTATION

Implementing AI in your business requires a strategic approach to measuring success. It is crucial to define specific success metrics that align with your organization's goals and objectives. When crafting these metrics, consider the unique aspects of AI technology and how it can drive value in your operations, products, or services. Some examples of success metrics include increased efficiency, cost savings, improved customer satisfaction, and enhanced decision-making capabilities.

Begin by identifying the key areas where AI can make the most significant impact and set measurable targets for each. It's essential to establish both short-term and long-term goals, as AI-driven initiatives often take time to fully realize their potential. Moreover, make sure that your success metrics are adaptable and can evolve as your business grows and changes. By setting clear and achievable targets, you can effectively track the progress of your AI implementation, identify areas for improvement, and ensure that your investment in AI technology pays off.

THE ART OF CONTINUOUS MONITORING AND ADJUSTING AI STRATEGIES

In the ever-evolving world of AI, it is essential for entrepreneurs to continuously monitor and adjust their AI strategies to stay ahead of the curve. AI technologies are constantly improving and changing, which means that businesses must be agile and ready to adapt in order to maintain a competitive edge.

Start by establishing a regular review process for your AI initiatives. This can involve tracking the performance of your AI systems, assessing their impact on your success metrics, and identifying any areas where improvements can be made. It's important to involve your team in these discussions, as they may provide valuable insights into the effectiveness of your AI solutions.

In addition to internal evaluations, stay informed about the latest developments in AI technology and industry best practices. By staying abreast of emerging trends, you can identify new opportunities to incorporate AI into your business processes or enhance your current AI systems.

As you make adjustments to your AI strategies, be prepared to iterate and refine them. It's not unusual for AI-driven projects to require some trial and error before achieving optimal results. Embrace the learning process, and remember that the key to success with AI is continuous improvement and adaptability. By regularly monitoring and adjusting your AI strategies, you can ensure your business stays on the cutting edge of technology and reaps the full benefits of AI-driven growth.

Evaluating the Return on Investment (ROI) of AI Initiatives

When implementing AI in your business, it's crucial to assess the return on investment (ROI) of these initiatives to ensure they're delivering value and contributing to your overall objectives. Evaluating ROI can help you make informed decisions about where to allocate resources and which AI projects to prioritize.

Begin by establishing clear goals and success metrics for each AI initiative. These can include both qualitative measures, such as improved customer satisfaction or enhanced decision-making, and quantitative measures, like cost savings, increased revenue, or reduced processing times. It's important to align these success metrics with your broader business objectives to ensure AI projects support your strategic goals.

Next, track the costs associated with each AI initiative. This should include both the upfront investment in AI technology, such as software and hardware, and the ongoing expenses related to maintenance, support, and system updates. Don't forget to account for the time and resources spent on training, implementation, and any necessary adjustments to your business processes.

Once you have established success metrics and tracked costs, compare the benefits of your AI initiatives with their associated expenses. Calculate the ROI by dividing the net benefit (i.e., the total benefits minus the costs) by the total costs. This will provide you with a clear understanding of the financial impact of each AI project and help you prioritize initiatives that offer the highest return.

Keep in mind that the ROI of AI initiatives may not be immediately apparent, as some benefits may take time to materialize. Be patient and continually assess the ROI of your AI projects over time. By regularly evaluating the return on investment of your AI initiatives, you can ensure your business is making the most of these cutting-edge technologies and driving sustainable growth.

FINAL THOUGHTS

As we conclude this chapter on measuring and tracking AI-driven success, it's essential to emphasize the importance of a comprehensive and ongoing evaluation process. Entrepreneurs must remain diligent in monitoring the performance of their AI initiatives, using defined success metrics and carefully considering the return on investment (ROI) for each project.

By establishing clear goals and aligning AI initiatives with broader business objectives, entrepreneurs can ensure their AI-driven projects contribute meaningfully to their organization's growth and success. Continuously monitoring and adjusting AI strategies based on real-world performance will help entrepreneurs adapt to market changes, improve their AI implementations, and maximize the benefits these technologies can offer.

Incorporating AI in your business is an exciting and transformative journey that can lead to a multitude of benefits, from cost savings to improved decision-making and enhanced customer experiences. By remaining focused on measuring and tracking the success of your AI-driven projects, you can ensure that your investment in these technologies is well-allocated and that your organization remains at the forefront of innovation in the rapidly evolving AI landscape.

CHAPTER 10

PREPARING FOR AI-DRIVEN INDUSTRY SHIFTS

IN THE DYNAMIC WORLD OF TECHNOLOGY AND INNOVATION, AI-driven industry shifts are becoming increasingly prevalent, transforming the way businesses operate and compete. As an entrepreneur, it is crucial to stay ahead of these changes and adapt your business strategies accordingly. In this chapter, we will delve into the importance of anticipating and preparing for AI-driven industry shifts, ensuring that your organization remains resilient, agile, and ready to embrace the opportunities that AI presents.

We will discuss the various ways in which AI is influencing industries, from automating processes to creating new business models and revolutionizing customer experiences. Additionally, we will provide practical tips and strategies for entrepreneurs to navigate the challenges posed by AI-driven disruptions, while capitalizing on the potential advantages that this technology can bring to the table. By understanding and preparing for AI-driven industry shifts, entrepreneurs can position their businesses for long-term success and stay at the forefront of their respective markets.

STAYING UPDATED ON AI ADVANCEMENTS AND TRENDS

As an entrepreneur navigating the rapidly evolving landscape of AI technology, it is essential to remain informed about the latest advancements and trends in the field. By staying updated on AI developments, you can ensure that your business stays competitive and capitalizes on the emerging opportunities that this technology presents. In this section, we will discuss several strategies for keeping up with AI advancements and trends, empowering you to make informed decisions about incorporating AI into your business.

One effective approach to staying current with AI advancements is by regularly following reputable news outlets, blogs, and research publications that cover AI and related topics. Industry conferences, webinars, and online courses can also provide valuable insights and knowledge on the latest AI trends and technologies. Additionally, engaging with AI-focused communities, such as forums, discussion groups, and social media platforms, can facilitate the exchange of ideas and experiences with other professionals and experts in the field.

Lastly, consider partnering with AI research organizations, universities, or startups that are actively working on cutting-edge AI technologies. These collaborations can provide direct access to the latest advancements in AI, as well as opportunities to implement and test these innovations within your own business. By staying informed about AI advancements and trends, entrepreneurs can make well-informed decisions and drive the success of their AI-driven initiatives.

ANTICIPATING AND ADAPTING TO REGULATORY CHANGES

As AI technology continues to evolve and permeate various aspects of our lives, governments and regulatory bodies are increasingly focused on establishing guidelines and policies to ensure its ethical and responsible use. Entrepreneurs must be proactive in anticipating and adapting to these regulatory changes to minimize potential risks and ensure long-term success. In this section, we will discuss strategies for staying abreast of regulatory developments in the AI domain and successfully integrating them into your business strategy.

First and foremost, make a conscious effort to stay informed about the latest AI-related regulations and policies on both national and international levels. Regularly follow news sources, industry publications, and governmental websites that provide updates on AI legislation and guidelines. Engaging with professional organizations, legal advisors, and industry associations can also help you better understand the implications of new regulations and the best practices for compliance.

As new regulations emerge, entrepreneurs must be prepared to adapt their AI-driven strategies and operations accordingly. This may involve updating data privacy policies, implementing new security measures, or adjusting AI algorithms to adhere to ethical guidelines. It is crucial to cultivate a culture of compliance within your organization by providing training and resources to employees, fostering open communication, and ensuring that your team understands the importance of adhering to AI-related regulations.

In addition to regulatory compliance, entrepreneurs should consider the potential public perception of their AI initiatives. Adopting a transparent approach and proactively addressing ethical concerns can help build trust with customers, investors, and other stakeholders. By anticipating and adapting to regulatory changes, entrepreneurs can ensure that their businesses remain compliant, competitive, and well-positioned to capitalize on the opportunities presented by AI technology.

DEVELOPING LONG-TERM STRATEGIES FOR AI-DRIVEN MARKET CHANGES

As AI technology continues to advance, it is essential for entrepreneurs to prepare for the inevitable market shifts that will result from widespread AI adoption. Developing long-term strategies to navigate these changes is crucial for businesses looking to stay competitive, seize opportunities, and thrive in an AI-driven world. In this section, we will discuss the key considerations for entrepreneurs in formulating and implementing long-term strategies that can help them adapt to AI-driven market changes.

One of the primary steps in developing long-term strategies is identifying the areas in your business where AI can create the most value. This involves assessing the potential impact of AI on your product or service offerings, operations, and customer interactions. By understanding how AI can enhance or disrupt your business, you can prioritize the areas where AI implementation will generate the most significant competitive advantage and allocate resources accordingly.

Another essential aspect of long-term strategic planning is fostering a culture of innovation and adaptability within your organization. Encourage your team to stay updated on the latest AI advancements and trends, and create an environment that supports experimentation and learning. Continuous improvement and a willingness to embrace change are key to thriving in an AI-driven market landscape.

Monitoring the competitive landscape is also crucial when formulating long-term strategies. Keep a close eye on how your competitors are leveraging AI technology and be prepared to respond to new innovations or market disruptions. This may involve forming strategic partnerships, investing in research and development, or acquiring AI-focused startups to enhance your capabilities and maintain a competitive edge.

In addition, entrepreneurs must consider the ethical implications of AI implementation in their long-term strategies. As AI technology becomes more prevalent, businesses will increasingly be expected to adhere to ethical guidelines and demonstrate responsible AI use. By prioritizing transparency, fairness, and accountability in your AI initiatives, you can build trust with customers, investors, and regulators.

Finally, regularly revisit and revise your long-term strategies as new AI technologies emerge and market dynamics evolve. This iterative approach will ensure that your business stays agile and ready to capitalize on the opportunities and challenges presented by AI-driven market changes. By proactively planning for the future, entrepreneurs can position their businesses for success in the ever-evolving AI landscape.

FINAL THOUGHTS

As we conclude this chapter, it is clear that the AI-driven future presents both opportunities and challenges for entrepreneurs. By understanding the implications of AI technology and proactively adapting to the changes it brings, businesses can leverage AI's transformative power to drive growth and success. Throughout this chapter, we have explored various aspects of preparing for AI-driven industry shifts, ranging from staying updated on advancements and trends to developing long-term strategies and anticipating regulatory changes.

The key takeaway for entrepreneurs is to adopt a forward-looking and adaptable mindset. Embracing AI technology and fostering a culture of innovation within your organization will help you navigate the rapidly evolving landscape and position your business for long-term success. By being proactive, informed, and strategic in your approach to AI, you can transform your business, outpace your competitors, and capitalize on the immense potential of AI-driven market changes.

As you continue your journey through this book, we hope that the insights and strategies provided will serve as a valuable guide for harnessing the power of AI in your entrepreneurial ventures. With the right mindset and approach, you can ensure that your business not only survives but thrives in the era of artificial intelligence.

CHAPTER 11

FOSTERING AN ETHICAL AND SUSTAINABLE AI-DRIVEN BUSINESS: INTRODUCTION

IN TODAY'S RAPIDLY EVOLVING TECHNOLOGICAL LANDSCAPE, businesses are increasingly leveraging artificial intelligence to drive innovation, efficiency, and competitive advantage. As entrepreneurs integrate AI into their operations, it is crucial to consider the ethical and sustainable implications of these technologies to ensure long-term success and responsible growth. In this chapter, we will explore the importance of fostering an ethical and sustainable AI-driven business, discussing the potential challenges and opportunities that entrepreneurs face in this endeavor.

We will delve into topics such as data privacy, fairness, transparency, and accountability, providing insights and guidance on how to build a business that is both technologically advanced and socially responsible. By prioritizing ethical considerations and adopting sustainable practices, entrepreneurs can create an AI-driven business that not only delivers value to customers and stakeholders but also contributes to the greater good. As you read through this chapter, we hope that you gain a deeper understanding of the importance of ethical and sustainable AI implementation and are inspired to take action in your own entrepreneurial journey.

Prioritizing Diversity and Inclusion in AI Development

Diversity and inclusion are essential components of ethical and sustainable AI-driven businesses. They ensure that the development and deployment of AI technologies consider the needs and perspectives of different individuals, communities, and cultures, thereby reducing the risk of unintended biases and promoting fairness. In this section, we will discuss the importance of prioritizing diversity and inclusion in AI development and provide actionable steps for entrepreneurs to integrate these principles into their businesses.

A diverse and inclusive AI development team can help identify and address potential biases in algorithms, data sets, and system outputs, leading to more accurate and equitable outcomes. By fostering a culture of diversity and inclusion, entrepreneurs can promote a sense of belonging among employees, increase creativity and innovation, and ultimately drive better decision-making. This can be achieved by adopting inclusive recruitment practices, offering training and development opportunities, and creating channels for open communication and feedback.

Additionally, entrepreneurs must be aware of the potential biases embedded in AI systems and work to mitigate their effects. This involves collecting and processing data responsibly, ensuring that it is representative of diverse populations, and regularly evaluating and adjusting AI models to minimize biases. Entrepreneurs can also collaborate with external organizations, including research institutions and community groups, to gain insights and feedback on their AI systems from diverse perspectives.

Prioritizing diversity and inclusion in AI development is crucial for creating ethical and sustainable AI-driven businesses. By embracing these principles, entrepreneurs can build more equitable technologies that serve the needs of all users and foster a positive impact on society as a whole.

DEVELOPING AI SOLUTIONS WITH A FOCUS ON SOCIAL IMPACT

As entrepreneurs leverage AI to drive innovation and growth, it is essential to consider the social impact of these technologies. By developing AI solutions that prioritize social good, businesses can contribute to solving pressing societal challenges while also building trust and fostering positive brand associations. In this section, we will discuss the importance of developing AI solutions with a focus on social impact and provide guidance for entrepreneurs on how to integrate this approach into their business strategies.

To develop AI solutions that drive social impact, entrepreneurs must first identify the issues that align with their business objectives and target market. This could include areas such as education, healthcare, sustainability, or social justice. By focusing on these specific issues, entrepreneurs can better understand the needs of affected communities and develop AI technologies that provide meaningful solutions.

Next, entrepreneurs should engage in a collaborative and inclusive process that involves various stakeholders, including domain experts, community representatives, and end-users. This approach ensures that AI solutions are designed to address real-world problems and are sensitive to the unique needs and values of the communities they serve. Entrepreneurs should also be transparent about their intentions and progress, fostering trust and accountability.

Moreover, it is vital to measure the social impact of AI solutions, tracking their effectiveness and adjusting them as needed. This can be achieved through a combination of quantitative and qualitative assessments that capture both the tangible outcomes and the broader effects on communities and individuals. By continuously evaluating their AI technologies, entrepreneurs can optimize their social impact and ensure that their solutions remain relevant and effective over time.

Developing AI solutions with a focus on social impact is

a powerful way for entrepreneurs to drive positive change while also fostering trust and credibility. By identifying relevant social issues, engaging in a collaborative development process, and measuring the impact of their AI technologies, entrepreneurs can create AI-driven businesses that not only achieve commercial success but also contribute to a better future for all.

BALANCING PROFIT AND PURPOSE IN AN AI-DRIVEN BUSINESS

In the rapidly evolving landscape of AI-driven businesses, entrepreneurs often grapple with striking the right balance between profit and purpose. While the pursuit of profitability is essential for the survival and growth of any business, it is equally important to consider the broader implications of AI technologies on society and the environment. In this section, we will explore strategies for entrepreneurs to balance profit and purpose in their AI-driven ventures, ensuring long-term success and a positive impact on the world.

To effectively balance profit and purpose, entrepreneurs should begin by defining a clear mission and set of values that guide their AI-driven business. This mission should encompass both the financial objectives and the broader goals related to social and environmental impact. By clearly articulating this dual focus, entrepreneurs can ensure that their business decisions align with their overarching purpose and values.

Next, entrepreneurs should integrate social and environmental considerations into their AI development processes. This can involve conducting impact assessments, engaging in stakeholder consultations, and implementing ethical guidelines for AI design and deployment. By proactively addressing potential risks and negative consequences, entrepreneurs can create AI-driven products and services that not only generate revenue but also contribute to social good.

Another essential strategy for balancing profit and purpose is to establish a culture of innovation and continuous learning. By fostering an environment that encourages experimentation, entrepreneurs can identify new opportunities for both financial growth and social impact. This includes staying up-to-date with the latest advancements in AI research, engaging with industry peers and experts, and embracing a mindset of adaptability and resilience.

Additionally, entrepreneurs should consider pursuing collaborations and partnerships with like-minded organizations. By aligning with other businesses, nonprofits, and research institutions that share similar goals, AI-driven ventures can leverage collective resources and expertise to amplify their impact and achieve greater profitability.

Finally, entrepreneurs should communicate their commitment to balancing profit and purpose to their customers, employees, and investors. By being transparent about their goals and progress, AI-driven businesses can foster trust, loyalty, and engagement from their stakeholders, ultimately contributing to long-term success and sustainable growth.

Balancing profit and purpose in an AI-driven business is a multifaceted endeavor that requires a clear mission, a proactive approach to ethical development, and a commitment to innovation and collaboration. By integrating these strategies into their business models, entrepreneurs can build successful AI-driven ventures that not only generate profit but also make a meaningful difference in the world.

Final Thoughts

As we conclude this chapter on fostering an ethical and sustainable AI-driven business, it is evident that embracing ethical principles, prioritizing diversity and inclusion, focusing on social impact, and balancing profit and purpose are key to long-term success. Entrepreneurs must remain vigilant and adaptable, understanding that their AI-driven businesses have the potential to shape the future in profound ways.

Emphasizing the importance of ethical considerations in AI development, entrepreneurs can create innovative products and services that not only drive business growth but also contribute positively to society. By embracing a mission-driven approach, entrepreneurs can ensure their AI-driven businesses are purposeful and sustainable, paving the way for continued success in a rapidly evolving technological landscape.

To truly thrive, entrepreneurs must be willing to invest in diverse talent, learn from industry experts, and engage in collaborations that drive innovation and positive change. By fostering a culture of learning, experimentation, and resilience, AI-driven businesses can overcome challenges and seize opportunities in a rapidly shifting environment.

As AI continues to advance and permeate various aspects of our lives, it is crucial for entrepreneurs to lead the way in shaping a future that is not only profitable but also ethical, inclusive, and sustainable. By following the strategies and principles discussed in this chapter, entrepreneurs can be at the forefront of creating AI-driven businesses that are a force for good in the world.

Chapter 12

Success Stories: Entrepreneurs Leveraging AI for Growth and Innovation

In this chapter, we will dive into a collection of inspiring success stories that showcase how entrepreneurs from various industries have harnessed the power of artificial intelligence (AI) to fuel their business growth and drive innovation. These case studies will not only provide valuable insights into the strategies and tactics employed by these innovative entrepreneurs, but also serve as motivation and inspiration for those looking to integrate AI into their own businesses.

The entrepreneurs featured in this chapter come from diverse backgrounds and industries, but they all share a common passion for leveraging AI to solve problems, create new opportunities, and disrupt traditional business models. From healthcare and agriculture to finance and marketing, these success stories highlight the transformative impact of AI on businesses of all sizes and sectors.

By examining these real-life examples, you will gain a deeper understanding of the immense potential of AI to revolutionize your business, helping you to identify areas where AI can create value and drive growth in your own entrepreneurial journey.

INSPIRING CASE STUDIES OF AI-DRIVEN ENTREPRENEURIAL VENTURES

In this section, we will explore a variety of inspiring case studies that demonstrate the transformative power of AI in entrepreneurial ventures across diverse industries. These examples will provide valuable insights into the innovative applications of AI and showcase the positive impact it can have on business growth and success.

1. HEALTHCARE: ZEBRA MEDICAL VISION, A STARTUP founded by Eyal Gura and Eyal Toledano, utilizes AI to analyze medical imaging data to assist in early detection of diseases. By leveraging deep learning algorithms, Zebra's platform can quickly and accurately identify anomalies in radiological scans, helping doctors make more informed decisions and potentially saving lives.

. . .

2. AGRICULTURE: FOUNDED BY JORGE HERAUD AND LEE Redden, Blue River Technology uses AI-driven robotics to revolutionize farming practices. Their flagship product, See & Spray, utilizes computer vision and machine learning to identify and selectively target weeds in real-time, reducing herbicide use by up to 90% and significantly lowering environmental impact.

3. FINANCE: KABBAGE, CO-FOUNDED BY ROB FROHWEIN AND Kathryn Petralia, is an AI-powered platform that provides small businesses with quick access to working capital through automated underwriting and risk assessment. By analyzing non-traditional data sources and using machine learning algorithms, Kabbage can make faster and more accurate lending decisions, helping small businesses thrive.

4. MARKETING: PERSADO, FOUNDED BY ALEX VRATSKIDES and Assaf Baciu, leverages AI to optimize marketing communications by analyzing language, emotions, and context. Their platform generates tailored messages that resonate with consumers, leading to improved engagement and higher conversion rates.

5. MANUFACTURING: CO-FOUNDED BY AMAR HANSPAL AND JF Brandon, Bright Machines is an AI-driven company that

helps manufacturers automate assembly lines through the use of smart robotics. Their AI-powered platform streamlines the production process, improves efficiency, and reduces the potential for human error, revolutionizing the way products are made.

THESE INSPIRING CASE STUDIES DEMONSTRATE THE VAST potential of AI to transform industries and empower entrepreneurs to develop innovative solutions that address real-world problems. By harnessing the power of AI, these visionary leaders have managed to create disruptive businesses that are redefining their industries and paving the way for a brighter future.

LESSONS LEARNED FROM AI-FOCUSED ENTREPRENEURS

AI-focused entrepreneurs have pioneered the use of cutting-edge technology to drive innovation and growth in their businesses. By examining their journeys and experiences, we can extract valuable lessons that can inform and inspire other entrepreneurs looking to leverage AI in their ventures.

1. EMBRACE A LEARNING MINDSET: AI IS A RAPIDLY evolving field, and staying up-to-date with the latest advancements is crucial for success. AI-focused entrepre-

neurs continually invest in their learning, whether by attending conferences, reading research papers, or participating in online courses. Embracing this mindset will ensure that you remain competitive in the ever-changing landscape of AI.

2. FOCUS ON SOLVING REAL-WORLD PROBLEMS: SUCCESSFUL AI-driven businesses are rooted in a deep understanding of the problems they aim to solve. By focusing on real-world issues and addressing genuine customer pain points, AI entrepreneurs can create solutions that have a meaningful impact and drive long-term value.

3. COLLABORATE WITH DIVERSE TALENT: AI DEVELOPMENT requires a diverse range of skills, from data science and engineering to domain-specific expertise. Successful AI entrepreneurs recognize the importance of assembling a multidisciplinary team, fostering a collaborative environment, and leveraging the unique strengths of each team member.

4. THINK LONG-TERM AND BE ADAPTABLE: THE DYNAMIC nature of AI means that businesses must be prepared to adapt to new technologies and market shifts. Entrepreneurs should develop long-term strategies that consider the poten-

tial implications of AI-driven changes, while also remaining flexible and responsive to emerging trends.

5. Prioritize ethical considerations: As AI continues to permeate various aspects of society, ethical concerns around data privacy, transparency, and fairness become increasingly important. AI entrepreneurs must take these issues seriously and strive to develop responsible, ethical solutions that take into account the broader implications of their technology.

6. Embrace failure and iterate: As with any entrepreneurial venture, success in the AI space often comes after multiple iterations and learning from failure. Entrepreneurs should be prepared to take risks, experiment, and learn from their setbacks in order to refine their AI-driven solutions and achieve success.

By taking these lessons to heart, entrepreneurs can effectively navigate the complex world of AI and create innovative, successful businesses that leverage the transformative power of this technology.

STRATEGIES FOR ADOPTING AI IN YOUR ENTREPRENEURIAL JOURNEY

Adopting AI in your entrepreneurial journey can be a game-changer, opening up new opportunities for innovation, efficiency, and growth. To successfully harness the power of AI, it is crucial to develop a strategic approach that aligns with your business goals and objectives. Here are some key strategies to consider as you embark on your AI-driven entrepreneurial journey:

1. ASSESS YOUR NEEDS AND SET CLEAR OBJECTIVES: BEGIN BY identifying the specific areas of your business that can benefit from AI integration. Evaluate the problems you want to address and set clear, measurable objectives to guide your AI adoption strategy.

2. EDUCATE YOURSELF AND YOUR TEAM: INVEST IN BUILDING your knowledge of AI technologies and their applications in your industry. Encourage your team to develop relevant skills and expertise, either through training programs or self-learning resources.

3. START SMALL AND SCALE UP: WHEN IMPLEMENTING AI, it's wise to start with small, focused projects that can deliver

quick wins and provide valuable insights. As you gain experience and confidence, you can gradually scale up your AI initiatives and tackle more complex challenges.

4. PRIORITIZE DATA QUALITY AND MANAGEMENT: AI THRIVES on high-quality data. Invest in building a robust data infrastructure and ensure your data is clean, accurate, and up-to-date. Implement strong data governance practices to maintain the integrity and privacy of your data.

5. COLLABORATE WITH EXPERTS AND PARTNERS: Establishing partnerships with AI experts, research organizations, or other businesses in the AI ecosystem can help you access valuable resources and knowledge. Collaborative projects can also lead to innovative solutions that drive mutual growth.

6. BE AGILE AND ADAPTIVE: AI IS A RAPIDLY EVOLVING FIELD, and your strategies should be agile and adaptive to changing technologies and market conditions. Regularly review your AI initiatives and be prepared to pivot or iterate based on new insights or developments.

. . .

7. MONITOR PROGRESS AND MEASURE SUCCESS: ESTABLISH performance metrics to track the impact of your AI projects on your business objectives. Continuously monitor progress and use data-driven insights to refine your strategies and optimize results.

8. MAINTAIN AN ETHICAL FOCUS: AS YOU INTEGRATE AI into your business, prioritize ethical considerations such as transparency, fairness, and data privacy. Develop responsible AI solutions that respect user rights and contribute positively to society.

BY FOLLOWING THESE STRATEGIES, YOU CAN EFFECTIVELY navigate the complexities of AI adoption and leverage its transformative potential to drive growth and success in your entrepreneurial journey.

FINAL THOUGHTS

As we conclude this chapter on the inspiring success stories of AI-driven entrepreneurship, it is clear that the integration of AI technologies has the power to revolutionize the way businesses operate, innovate, and grow. By learning from the experiences of those who have successfully harnessed AI, entrepreneurs can gain valuable insights and inspiration to guide their own AI-driven journey.

The key takeaways from this chapter underscore the importance of strategic planning, collaboration, adaptability, and ethical considerations when embracing AI. Adopting these best practices will help entrepreneurs navigate the challenges and complexities of AI adoption while maximizing the potential benefits.

In the rapidly evolving world of AI, staying informed, agile, and open to collaboration is vital. By continuously learning from the experiences of others and refining their strategies, entrepreneurs can harness the transformative power of AI to create new opportunities, drive innovation, and unlock untapped potential in their businesses.

As we move forward, it is essential to remember that AI technologies are tools designed to augment human capabilities and empower entrepreneurs to achieve greater success. By embracing AI in a responsible and strategic manner, entrepreneurs can pave the way for a brighter, more efficient, and sustainable future in the world of business.

Conclusion

The Future of Entrepreneurship and AI - A Synergistic Partnership

As we reach the conclusion of this comprehensive guide for entrepreneurs on AI for their businesses, it is essential to reflect on the profound impact AI technologies have on the future of entrepreneurship. The transformative power of AI has the potential to reshape industries, redefine business models, and create new opportunities for innovation and growth. By understanding and embracing the possibilities offered by AI, entrepreneurs can stay ahead of the curve and navigate the fast-paced, ever-changing landscape of modern business.

The dynamic partnership between entrepreneurship and AI is a testament to the synergistic relationship between human ingenuity and technological advancement. The adoption of AI in various aspects of business operations, from market research to product development, empowers entrepreneurs to streamline processes, enhance efficiency, and make more informed decisions. By leveraging AI, entrepreneurs can focus on driving innovation, fostering creativity, and pursuing their vision with renewed determination and confidence.

As we look toward the future, it is crucial for entrepreneurs to remain agile and adaptable in the face of constant change. Staying informed about the latest AI advancements, engaging with AI-focused communities, and nurturing an innovation-centric mindset will enable entrepreneurs to harness the power of AI and thrive in the increasingly competitive global market.

Ultimately, the future of entrepreneurship and AI is one of collaboration and mutual growth. By integrating AI technologies with human expertise, creativity, and passion, entrepreneurs can unlock new opportunities, overcome challenges, and contribute to a better, more prosperous world for all.

The Evolving Role of AI in Entrepreneurship - Shaping the Future of Business

As AI continues to advance and permeate various aspects of our lives, its role in entrepreneurship is also evolving at an unprecedented pace. The transformative power of AI technologies is not only redefining the way businesses operate, but also shaping the future of entrepreneurship itself. In this new landscape, entrepreneurs must recognize the potential of AI to drive innovation, improve decision-making, and unlock untapped opportunities.

One of the most significant aspects of the evolving role of AI in entrepreneurship is its capacity to democratize access to cutting-edge technologies. By leveling the playing field, AI enables startups and small businesses to compete with established corporations, fostering a more inclusive and dynamic entrepreneurial ecosystem. Through the use of AI-driven tools and platforms, entrepreneurs can access valuable insights, automate processes, and improve efficiency, regardless of their size or resources.

Furthermore, AI is revolutionizing the way entrepreneurs approach problem-solving and decision-making. By leveraging machine learning algorithms and advanced data analytics, entrepreneurs can make more informed decisions, identify patterns and trends, and predict future outcomes with greater accuracy. This data-driven approach enables entrepreneurs to better understand their customers, optimize their products and services, and discover new market opportunities.

The evolving role of AI in entrepreneurship also extends to its potential to spur innovation and foster creativity. By automating routine tasks and streamlining workflows, AI frees up time for entrepreneurs to focus on higher-level thinking, ideation, and strategic planning. In addition, AI-powered tools can enhance collaboration, facilitate communication, and promote the sharing of ideas, fostering a culture of innovation within organizations.

As AI continues to reshape the entrepreneurial landscape, it is essential for entrepreneurs to adapt and evolve alongside it. By embracing the potential of AI and integrating it into their businesses, entrepreneurs can unlock new opportunities for growth, innovation, and success, shaping the future of entrepreneurship for years to come.

Seizing the Moment: Encouraging Entrepreneurs to Embrace AI-Driven Opportunities

As the world undergoes a technological revolution driven by artificial intelligence (AI), it is essential for entrepreneurs to embrace the myriad of opportunities presented by this transformation. By integrating AI into their businesses, entrepreneurs can gain a competitive edge, optimize their operations, and unlock new avenues for growth and innovation.

Firstly, entrepreneurs should acknowledge the potential of AI to disrupt traditional industries and create entirely new markets. By leveraging AI-driven solutions, entrepreneurs can tap into unexplored niches and uncover new business opportunities that might have been previously inaccessible. AI can help entrepreneurs anticipate and adapt to emerging trends, ensuring their businesses remain relevant and at the forefront of their respective sectors.

Moreover, entrepreneurs must recognize the value of AI in streamlining processes, enhancing productivity, and reducing operational costs. By automating repetitive tasks, optimizing workflows, and improving decision-making, AI enables entrepreneurs to focus on higher-level strategic planning, innovation, and business development. This shift not only drives growth but also fosters a culture of creativity and collaboration within organizations.

Another essential aspect of embracing AI-driven opportunities is the importance of fostering a data-driven mindset. Entrepreneurs should strive to harness the power of data analytics and AI algorithms to gain deeper insights into customer behavior, market dynamics, and industry trends. By leveraging these insights, entrepreneurs can make informed decisions, tailor their products and services to meet customer needs, and drive continuous improvement.

Lastly, entrepreneurs should actively participate in AI-focused communities, collaborate with research organizations, and engage with industry leaders. By immersing themselves in the AI ecosystem, entrepreneurs can stay informed about the latest AI advancements, exchange ideas with like-minded individuals, and gain access to valuable resources, partnerships, and support networks.

The rapidly evolving AI landscape offers entrepreneurs

a wealth of opportunities for growth, innovation, and success. By embracing AI-driven solutions and adopting a forward-thinking mindset, entrepreneurs can position their businesses for long-term prosperity in an increasingly competitive and AI-driven world.

Laying the Foundation: Setting the Stage for a Successful AI-Powered Entrepreneurial Journey

As AI continues to reshape the landscape of entrepreneurship, it is crucial for business owners to set the stage for a successful AI-powered journey. By adopting a strategic and proactive approach, entrepreneurs can effectively leverage AI to transform their businesses and drive growth.

First and foremost, entrepreneurs need to develop a clear understanding of the AI technologies relevant to their industry and business model. This involves staying abreast of the latest AI advancements, trends, and best practices, as well as identifying potential use cases and applications that align with their specific needs and objectives. By doing so, entrepreneurs can create a solid foundation for integrating AI into their operations and gaining a competitive edge.

Next, entrepreneurs must invest in building an AI-driven team that includes a diverse mix of experts, ranging from data scientists and engineers to domain specialists and business strategists. This team should work collaboratively to design, develop, and implement AI solutions that address pressing business challenges and drive value. Additionally, it is essential to foster a culture of innovation and learning within the organization, encouraging team members to continually explore new AI applications and improve existing ones.

Another critical aspect of setting the stage for a successful AI-powered journey is to establish a robust data infrastructure. Entrepreneurs should prioritize the collection, management, and analysis of high-quality data, as this serves as the lifeblood of AI-driven systems. By ensuring data is accurate, relevant, and representative, entrepreneurs can enhance the performance and reliability of their AI solutions, leading to more accurate insights and better decision-making.

Moreover, entrepreneurs must be mindful of the ethical and sustainable dimensions of AI, striving to develop solutions that prioritize diversity, inclusion, and social impact. By adopting a responsible and purpose-driven approach to AI, entrepreneurs can not only create value for their business but also contribute positively to society at large.

Lastly, it is crucial for entrepreneurs to maintain a growth mindset and remain agile in the face of AI-driven industry shifts. This includes continually reassessing and refining AI strategies, adapting to changing market conditions, and embracing new opportunities as they emerge.

Setting the stage for a successful AI-powered entrepreneurial journey requires a holistic and strategic approach. By developing a deep understanding of AI technologies, building a diverse and skilled team, establishing a strong data infrastructure, and fostering an ethical and innovative culture, entrepreneurs can unlock the full potential of AI to transform their businesses and chart a course for lasting success.

50 Prompts for AI for Entrepreneurs

As artificial intelligence (AI) continues to gain momentum and become increasingly integrated into our daily lives, it has become a key driver of innovation and growth for entrepreneurs. AI has the potential to transform industries and create new opportunities for businesses of all sizes, from improving customer experiences and optimizing operations to creating new products and services. However, with so much potential, it can be difficult for entrepreneurs to know where to start with AI. That's why we've compiled this appendix of 50 prompts for AI for entrepreneurs, covering a range of advanced topics that can help entrepreneurs effectively leverage AI in their businesses. Whether you're just starting to explore the potential of AI or you're already well-versed in the technology, these prompts can provide valuable insights and strategies for creating a successful AI strategy.

1. What are some advanced growth strategies that entrepreneurs can use to scale their startups rapidly while maintaining profitability, such as strategic partnerships, mergers and acquisitions, and international expansion? Additionally, how can entrepreneurs effectively measure and analyze key performance metrics to track growth and make informed decisions?

2. How can entrepreneurs leverage emerging technologies like artificial intelligence, machine learning, and predictive analytics to conduct more sophisticated market research, identify target customers more accurately, and create personalized marketing campaigns that maximize ROI?

3. What are some advanced strategies for mitigating risk and avoiding common pitfalls in entrepreneurship, such as conducting market experiments, building a diverse team with complementary skill sets, and cultivating a culture of innovation and adaptability? Additionally, how can entrepreneurs optimize their decision-making processes and cultivate a growth mindset to navigate challenges and capitalize on opportunities?

4. How can entrepreneurs use advanced branding techniques like experiential marketing, storytelling,

and emotional branding to create a deeper connection with customers and foster brand loyalty? Additionally, how can entrepreneurs use data and analytics to measure the effectiveness of their branding efforts and adjust their strategy accordingly?

5. What are some advanced funding strategies that entrepreneurs can use to secure funding from institutional investors like private equity firms and family offices, and how can entrepreneurs prepare for the due diligence process and negotiate favorable terms? Additionally, how can entrepreneurs build a strong financial foundation for their business by managing cash flow, forecasting financials, and creating a robust financial plan?

6. How can entrepreneurs develop a sustainable and socially responsible business model that balances profitability with social and environmental impact, and what are some innovative ways to measure and communicate this impact to stakeholders?

7. How can entrepreneurs use data analytics and business intelligence tools to optimize their operations and increase efficiency, and what are some key performance indicators (KPIs) that entrepreneurs should track to measure success?

8. What are some advanced techniques for building a strong company culture that attracts and retains top talent, fosters collaboration and creativity, and

supports diversity, equity, and inclusion (DEI) initiatives?

9. How can entrepreneurs effectively manage intellectual property (IP) and navigate legal issues related to patents, trademarks, and copyrights, especially in the context of global markets and emerging technologies?

10. What are some advanced strategies for creating a successful exit plan, such as mergers and acquisitions, initial public offerings (IPOs), and management buyouts, and how can entrepreneurs prepare for a successful exit while ensuring the long-term success of their business?

11. How can entrepreneurs use design thinking and human-centered design methodologies to create products and services that meet the needs and preferences of their target customers, and what are some best practices for testing and iterating on these solutions?

12. What are some advanced techniques for creating a strong omnichannel customer experience that integrates online and offline touchpoints, and how can entrepreneurs use data and analytics to measure and optimize this experience?

13. How can entrepreneurs leverage emerging technologies like blockchain, the Internet of Things (IoT), and augmented reality (AR) to create innova-

tive business models and disrupt traditional industries?

14. What are some advanced sales and marketing strategies that entrepreneurs can use to generate leads, close deals, and drive revenue growth, such as account-based marketing, sales enablement, and customer relationship management (CRM)?

15. What are some advanced strategies for building a resilient and agile supply chain that can adapt to disruptions and changes in market demand, and how can entrepreneurs use data and analytics to optimize this supply chain?

16. How can entrepreneurs effectively manage risk and protect their business from cyber threats, fraud, and other forms of malicious activity, and what are some best practices for creating a strong cybersecurity posture?

17. What are some advanced strategies for international expansion, such as localization, cultural adaptation, and global branding, and how can entrepreneurs effectively navigate cultural differences and legal frameworks in different regions?

18. How can entrepreneurs create a successful e-commerce strategy that maximizes conversions and revenue, and what are some best practices for optimizing the customer journey and reducing cart abandonment?

19. What are some advanced strategies for creating a

high-performing team that can execute on the entrepreneur's vision and drive business growth, such as leadership development, talent acquisition, and performance management?

20. How can entrepreneurs create a sustainable and scalable business model that balances short-term profitability with long-term growth and impact, and what are some innovative financing models and investment vehicles that can support this model?

21. How can entrepreneurs use predictive analytics and machine learning to create a data-driven approach to product development, pricing, and customer segmentation, and what are some best practices for implementing these techniques?

22. What are some advanced strategies for creating a culture of innovation and entrepreneurship within an organization, such as hackathons, incubators, and accelerators, and how can entrepreneurs encourage employees to take risks and embrace change?

23. How can entrepreneurs effectively leverage social media and influencer marketing to build brand awareness and engagement, and what are some best practices for measuring and optimizing social media ROI?

24. What are some advanced techniques for building a successful content marketing strategy, such as creating multimedia content, repurposing content across different channels, and using artificial

intelligence to personalize content for different audiences?

25. How can entrepreneurs use agile methodologies and lean startup principles to optimize their business processes and adapt quickly to changing market conditions, and what are some best practices for implementing these frameworks?

26. What are some advanced strategies for creating a strong employer brand and attracting top talent, such as employer branding campaigns, employee advocacy programs, and employee value proposition (EVP) development?

27. How can entrepreneurs effectively manage and grow a remote workforce, and what are some best practices for fostering collaboration, communication, and productivity in a virtual environment?

28. What are some advanced techniques for creating a successful product launch, such as pre-launch marketing campaigns, early adopter programs, and user testing, and how can entrepreneurs effectively measure and optimize product performance post-launch?

29. How can entrepreneurs create a successful customer retention strategy that maximizes lifetime customer value and reduces churn, and what are some best practices for creating a loyal customer base?

30. What are some advanced techniques for

measuring and optimizing business performance, such as balanced scorecards, lean metrics, and key predictive indicators (KPIs), and how can entrepreneurs use these metrics to inform business decisions and drive growth?

31. How can entrepreneurs use data and analytics to identify and capitalize on emerging market trends, and what are some advanced techniques for analyzing market data, such as sentiment analysis, trend mapping, and social listening?

32. What are some advanced strategies for creating a successful B2B sales and marketing strategy, such as account-based marketing, lead nurturing, and customer journey mapping, and how can entrepreneurs effectively measure and optimize this strategy?

33. How can entrepreneurs effectively manage and optimize their cash flow, and what are some advanced techniques for forecasting financials, reducing expenses, and generating additional revenue streams?

34. What are some advanced strategies for creating a successful customer experience that exceeds expectations, such as personalized customer service, gamification, and loyalty programs, and how can entrepreneurs effectively measure and optimize this experience?

35. How can entrepreneurs effectively manage risk and create a comprehensive risk management plan,

including identifying potential risks, assessing their impact and likelihood, and creating risk mitigation strategies?

36. What are some advanced techniques for creating a successful product roadmap and aligning product development with business strategy, such as agile product management, lean product development, and design thinking?

37. How can entrepreneurs use emerging technologies like virtual and augmented reality, voice search, and chatbots to create innovative customer experiences and disrupt traditional industries?

38. What are some advanced strategies for creating a strong company culture that fosters innovation, creativity, and employee engagement, such as creating a learning organization, promoting diversity and inclusion, and implementing employee recognition programs?

39. How can entrepreneurs create a successful thought leadership strategy that establishes them as industry experts and drives brand awareness and engagement, such as publishing original research, speaking at industry events, and engaging with the media?

40. What are some advanced techniques for creating a successful partnership strategy, such as identifying strategic partners, negotiating favorable terms, and

measuring the impact of partnerships on business growth?

41. What are some advanced strategies for creating a successful SEO and SEM strategy, such as optimizing for voice search, using data-driven keyword research, and incorporating machine learning and natural language processing?

42. How can entrepreneurs create a successful customer advocacy program that leverages satisfied customers to drive referrals, reviews, and brand advocacy, and what are some best practices for measuring and optimizing this program?

43. What are some advanced techniques for creating a successful go-to-market strategy, such as product differentiation, pricing optimization, and multi-channel distribution, and how can entrepreneurs effectively measure and optimize this strategy?

44. How can entrepreneurs effectively manage intellectual property and navigate legal issues related to licensing, franchising, and joint ventures, especially in the context of global markets and emerging technologies?

45. What are some advanced strategies for creating a successful product design and development process, such as rapid prototyping, usability testing, and design sprints, and how can entrepreneurs effectively measure and optimize this process?

46. How can entrepreneurs create a successful

crowdfunding campaign that leverages the power of the crowd to raise capital and drive brand awareness, and what are some best practices for preparing a successful campaign?

47. What are some advanced strategies for creating a successful customer retention program that maximizes customer lifetime value and reduces churn, such as creating personalized content, using data-driven insights, and implementing loyalty programs?

48. How can entrepreneurs create a successful thought leadership program that establishes them as industry experts and drives brand awareness and engagement, such as creating original content, speaking at industry events, and engaging with influencers?

49. What are some advanced techniques for creating a successful pricing strategy, such as value-based pricing, dynamic pricing, and price optimization, and how can entrepreneurs effectively measure and optimize this strategy?

50. How can entrepreneurs create a successful innovation strategy that drives continuous improvement and generates new revenue streams, such as investing in research and development, fostering collaboration and experimentation, and implementing design thinking and agile methodologies?

50 Advanced Prompts for Entrepreneurs: Starting Your Business

As the business landscape becomes increasingly complex and competitive, entrepreneurs need to leverage the power of technology to stay ahead of the curve. From artificial intelligence and machine learning to big data analytics and automation, there are a myriad of tools and strategies that can help entrepreneurs improve operations, streamline processes, and create innovative products and services. However, for entrepreneurs who are just starting out or looking to take their business to the next level, navigating the vast and ever-evolving world of technology can be daunting. That's why we've compiled a list of advanced prompts specifically tailored to entrepreneurs, designed to help you develop and execute effective strategies that leverage the latest technology trends and best practices. These prompts cover a range of topics, from customer acquisition and retention to product development and intellectual property management, and can help you achieve your business goals and succeed in today's fast-paced and dynamic marketplace.

1. What are some advanced strategies for market research and competitive analysis, such as using big data analytics and sentiment analysis to identify market trends and customer preferences?

2. How can entrepreneurs create a successful business plan that includes a comprehensive financial model and considers various scenarios and potential risks?

3. What are some advanced techniques for creating a strong brand identity and messaging, such as using psychographics and buyer personas to target specific audiences?

4. How can entrepreneurs create a successful go-to-market strategy, such as leveraging digital marketing channels and creating targeted campaigns that reach the right audience?

5. What are some advanced techniques for creating a strong customer acquisition strategy, such as using artificial intelligence to optimize lead generation and conversion rates?

6. How can entrepreneurs effectively manage cash flow and working capital, including forecasting and

managing expenses and creating a financial dash-
board that tracks key performance indicators?

7. What are some advanced techniques for creating a
strong sales process, such as using account-based
selling and creating a sales playbook that includes
objection handling and closing techniques?

8. How can entrepreneurs effectively manage people
and build a strong company culture, including
creating employee engagement programs and
fostering diversity and inclusion?

9. What are some advanced techniques for creating a
successful product launch, such as using digital
marketing and creating a pre-launch buzz to
generate interest and demand?

10. How can entrepreneurs create a successful
content marketing strategy that leverages different
channels and formats, such as creating original
content and repurposing it for different platforms?

11. What are some advanced techniques for building
and managing an effective team, such as using agile
methodologies and creating a performance management system that includes regular feedback and
coaching?

12. How can entrepreneurs create a strong customer
retention strategy, including using analytics to identify customer needs and preferences and creating
loyalty programs and referral campaigns?

13. What are some advanced techniques for creating

a successful partnership strategy, such as identifying strategic partners and creating mutually beneficial agreements?

14. How can entrepreneurs effectively manage their online reputation and brand perception, including monitoring social media and other online channels and creating a crisis management plan?

15. What are some advanced techniques for creating a successful pricing strategy, such as using dynamic pricing and creating value-based pricing models that take into account customer needs and preferences?

16. How can entrepreneurs create a strong lead generation and nurturing strategy, including using artificial intelligence to identify high-value leads and creating targeted campaigns that drive conversions?

17. What are some advanced techniques for creating a successful customer service experience, such as using artificial intelligence to automate support and creating a self-service portal that empowers customers?

18. How can entrepreneurs create a successful growth strategy, including using mergers and acquisitions and expanding into new markets and geographies?

19. What are some advanced techniques for creating a successful product design and development process, such as using agile methodologies and

creating a product roadmap that includes user testing and feedback?

20. How can entrepreneurs create a successful exit strategy, including using mergers and acquisitions and preparing for an initial public offering or other financing options?

21. What are some advanced techniques for creating a successful digital marketing strategy, such as using search engine optimization and pay-per-click advertising to drive traffic and conversions?

22. How can entrepreneurs create a successful social media strategy, including using influencer marketing and creating a content calendar that includes multimedia formats and user-generated content?

23. What are some advanced techniques for creating a successful mobile app development strategy, such as using artificial intelligence and creating a user experience that is optimized for mobile devices?

24. How can entrepreneurs create a successful product differentiation strategy, including using artificial intelligence to create unique features and benefits that set their product apart from competitors?

25. What are some advanced techniques for creating a successful e-commerce strategy, such as using artificial intelligence to optimize product recommendations and creating a seamless and efficient user experience for customers.

26. How can entrepreneurs create a successful

customer feedback and engagement strategy, including using social listening and creating feedback loops that incorporate customer input into product development?

27. What are some advanced techniques for creating a successful influencer marketing strategy, such as using artificial intelligence to identify optimal influencers and creating custom campaigns that drive engagement and conversions?

28. How can entrepreneurs create a successful customer journey and experience, including using artificial intelligence to personalize content and messaging at each stage of the customer journey?

29. What are some advanced techniques for creating a successful event marketing strategy, such as using artificial intelligence to optimize event planning and creating custom experiences that drive engagement and conversions?

30. How can entrepreneurs effectively manage their intellectual property, including creating patent and trademark portfolios and using legal strategies to protect their assets?

31. What are some advanced techniques for creating a successful investor pitch, including using data and analytics to support their business model and presenting a compelling story that resonates with investors?

32. How can entrepreneurs create a successful

employee training and development program, including using artificial intelligence to personalize training content and creating a culture of continuous learning and development?

33. What are some advanced techniques for creating a successful customer segmentation and targeting strategy, including using artificial intelligence to identify high-value customer segments and creating targeted campaigns that resonate with their needs and preferences?

34. How can entrepreneurs create a successful website design and user experience, including using artificial intelligence to optimize website layout, design, and navigation?

35. What are some advanced techniques for creating a successful product roadmap and backlog, including using agile methodologies and creating a product vision that aligns with customer needs and market trends?

36. How can entrepreneurs effectively manage their time and prioritize tasks, including using productivity tools and creating a routine that maximizes efficiency and focus?

37. What are some advanced techniques for creating a successful affiliate marketing strategy, including using artificial intelligence to optimize affiliate partnerships and creating custom campaigns that drive conversions?

38. How can entrepreneurs create a successful crisis management plan, including using artificial intelligence to monitor and respond to negative publicity and create a plan that addresses potential risks and threats?

39. What are some advanced techniques for creating a successful customer referral program, including using artificial intelligence to identify high-value customers and create custom campaigns that incentivize referrals?

40. How can entrepreneurs create a successful business model that takes into account revenue streams, cost structure, and competitive advantage, including using data and analytics to support their model and identify potential risks and challenges?

41. What are some advanced techniques for creating a successful product positioning and messaging, including using data and analytics to identify optimal messaging and creating a messaging hierarchy that resonates with different customer segments?

42. How can entrepreneurs create a successful thought leadership program that establishes them as industry experts and drives brand awareness and engagement, including using artificial intelligence to identify industry trends and create original content that adds value to the conversation?

43. What are some advanced techniques for creating a successful employee advocacy program, including

using artificial intelligence to personalize messaging and create a culture of employee engagement and participation?

44. How can entrepreneurs create a successful competitive analysis strategy, including using artificial intelligence to identify competitors and create a comprehensive analysis of their strengths, weaknesses, opportunities, and threats?

45. What are some advanced techniques for creating a successful business development strategy, including using data and analytics to identify new opportunities and create partnerships that drive growth and expansion?

46. How can entrepreneurs effectively manage their online presence and reputation, including using artificial intelligence to monitor social media and other online channels and create a strategy that addresses potential risks and challenges?

47. What are some advanced techniques for creating a successful customer lifetime value strategy, including using artificial intelligence to identify high-value customers and create a plan that maximizes their lifetime value to the business?

48. How can entrepreneurs create a successful customer advocacy program, including using artificial intelligence to identify high-value advocates and create a strategy that leverages their influence and drives brand advocacy and referrals?

49. What are some advanced techniques for creating a successful email automation strategy, including using artificial intelligence to personalize messaging and create automated campaigns that drive engagement and conversions?

50. How can entrepreneurs create a successful product expansion strategy, including using data and analytics to identify new product opportunities and create a plan that maximizes revenue and market share?

ABOUT JAMIE CULICAN
AUTHOR, MARKETER, PUBLISHER, TEACHER

Jamie is a USA Today bestselling author with a passion for helping other authors succeed. She is the owner of Dragon Realm Press, a publishing house that specializes in working with indie authors. With over a decade of experience in the publishing industry, Jamie has become an expert in book marketing, book design, and book editing. Her approach is centered on creating a personalized and collaborative experience for her clients that results in high-quality, marketable books.

Her extensive marketing background allows her to guide authors through the complex world of book promotion, providing them with strategies that work. Jamie believes that every author has a unique voice, and she is committed to helping them share their stories with the world.

With a focus on innovation, Jamie has been at the forefront of integrating AI into the publishing industry. She believes that AI is a powerful tool that can help authors streamline their processes and reach new audiences. Jamie is passionate about helping authors navigate the ever-changing landscape of publishing and achieve their goals.

ABOUT MELLE MELKUMIAN
AUTHOR, TECHNOLOGIST, MARKETER, PUBLISHER

Melle has spent her career translating complex technology for the lay person, working with prestigious organizations such as NASA, Northrop Grumman, and Hewlett Packard. As the Marketing Director for an AI-enabled app company, Melle continues to leverage technology to drive meaningful change. She believes we are at a pivotal moment in history, where the incredible potential of AI is set to revolutionize the way we work and live. Melle is passionate about helping people navigate this shift and harness the power of AI to achieve their goals. Her expertise and unique perspective make her an invaluable resource for anyone looking to tap into the full potential of AI in their personal or professional life.

Outside of her professional career, Melle is a USA Today bestselling author, having published multiple books with rave reviews through a fresh approach to fantasy story-telling. Through her work as an author, Melle has gained a deep understanding of the writing and publishing process, and how emerging technologies like AI can support and enhance the creative process. She is excited to share her expertise and insights with fellow authors in the AI for Authors community.

About AI4CES
Empowering Professionals, Transforming Industries

AI4CES, the AI-focused educational platform designed to empower individuals across a wide range of vertical markets, including publishing, proposal and grant writing, and education. With our mission to make AI accessible to everyone, we provide comprehensive, tailored learning experiences through online classes, webinars, and more. Our expertly crafted courses break down complex AI concepts into digestible, easy-to-understand lessons, enabling you to harness the power of AI and revolutionize the way you work in your industry.

Don't miss the opportunity to stay ahead in today's competitive landscape by mastering AI with AI4CES. Our adaptive, engaging, and interactive learning modules ensure that you receive personalized, cutting-edge education in a format that suits your needs and preferences. Join the AI revolution with AI4CES and transform the way you approach challenges in your profession, from publishing to grant writing and beyond.

www.AI4CES.com

www.ingramcontent.com/pod-product-compliance
Lightning Source LLC
Chambersburg PA
CBHW060843220526
45466CB00003B/1216